LAUGHTER IS THE BEST MEDICINE!

A 2-in-1 Book Bundle with the 1000 Funniest Quotes to Make You Laugh, Relax, and Refresh!

Edited by Stan Hardy

Notice:

Please note that the information contained within this document is for entertainment purposes only. All effort has been made to present accurate and reliable information. The content within this book has been derived from various sources. By reading this document, the reader agrees that under no circumstances is the author responsible for any losses, direct or indirect, which are incurred as a result of the use of the information contained within this document, including, but not limited to, errors, omissions, or inaccuracies.

TABLE OF CONTENTS

500 FUNNY QUOTES FOR WOMEN

Inspirational Quotes to Boost Your Mood Instantly & Make Your Day A Little Happier!

Edited by Stan Hardy

PREFACE

Humor sticks the most with people, especially when it is short and contains some truth or life lessons. That is why funny quotes are so great! They allow us to take a quick break, relax, and take life a bit easier. We can also draw inspiration from them, knowing that Albert Einstein, Ernest Hemingway, Charlie Chaplin, or some other great minds had the same experiences and struggles as ours.

This uplifting book provides 500 funny quotes with some of the universal truisms that are part of our everyday lives. The spectrum of quotes is as diverse as they are funny. Whether it is a quote about Relationships, Children, Age, Sports, Fun, People, or Religion, reading these can't help but make one smile, think, learn from their wisdom, chuckle, and refresh.

You can enjoy this book by reading it cover to cover or by going directly to your topic of interest. The quotes are carefully selected from various sources and thousands of quotes. All efforts have been made to check the quotes' source and to use the correct attributions. If you are looking for some quality, inspirational, and funny quotes to brighten your day, this is the book for you! If this book made you smile, please take the time to leave a review to help future readers like yourself and help me as a publisher. You might as well enjoy my other work with 500 funny quotes for men.

Thank you for your time. I hope you will have lots of fun!

Stan Hardy

Other Books by Dream Books LLC

Mark Twain Quotes of Wit and Wisdom

The Little book of Quotes for Festive Occasions

MEN, WOMEN & RELATIONSHIPS

Men marry women with the hope they will never change. Women marry men with the hope they will change. Invariably they are both disappointed.

Albert Einstein

I love being married. It's so great to find that one special person you want to annoy for the rest of your life.

Rita Rudner

We sleep in separate rooms, we have dinner apart, we take separate vacations – we're doing everything we can to keep our marriage together.

Rodney Dangerfield

Not sure which is harder on a relationship: sharing a dresser for three years or sharing an iPhone charger for one day.

Rhea Butcher

The useless piece of flesh at the end of a penis is called a man.

Jo Brand

I do not want people to be very agreeable, as it saves me the trouble of liking them a great deal.

One should always be in love. That is the reason one should never marry.

Oscar Wilde

I do not want people to be very agreeable, as it saves me the trouble of liking them a great deal.

Jane Austen

Never follow anyone else's path. Unless you're in the woods and you're lost and you see a path. Then by all means follow that path.

Ellen DeGeneres

Men are like shoes. Some fit better than others. And sometimes you go out shopping and there's nothing you like. And then, as luck would have it, the next week you find two that are perfect, but you don't have the money to buy both.

Janet Evanovich

I hate women because they always know where things are.

Voltaire

Never trust a man with testicles.

Jo Brand

I've come to learn that the best time to debate family members is when they have food in their mouths.

Kenneth Cole, fashion designer

I like the male body; it's better designed than the male mind.

Andrea Newman

Women have more imagination than men. They need it to tell us how wonderful we are.

Arnold H. Glasow

Diamonds never leave you – men do!

Shirley Bassey

A successful man is one who makes more money than his wife can spend. A successful woman is one who can find such a man.

Lana Turner

Women are wiser than men because they know less and understand more.

James Thurber

My father always said, 'Never trust anyone whose TV is bigger than their bookshelf.'

Emilia Clarke

Most of us women like men, you know; it's just that we find them a constant disappointment.

Clare Short

Being a woman is a terribly difficult task since it consists principally in dealing with men.

Joseph Conrad

Women give us solace, but if it were not for women we would never need solace.

Don Herold

Women can talk, empathize, apply lipstick, see things using the eyes in the back of their head, remember birthdays, write lists, run the country and bark demands, all while executing a spot of parallel parking.

Liz Jones

My feeling is that women will never be equal to men. I think men are catching up in all kinds of ways.

Jack Dee

Only fine cigars are worth smoking and only men who smoke fine cigars are worth kissing.

Joan Collins

Men think about women. Women think about what men think about them.

Peter Ustinov

We women talk too much, but even then we don't tell half what we know.

Nancy Astor

Men don't know much about women. We do know when they're happy. We know when they're crying, and we know when they're pissed off. We just don't know in what order these are gonna' come at us.

Evan Davies

When a man opens a car door for his wife, it's either a new car or a new wife.

Prince Philip

American husbands are the best in the world; no other husbands are so generous to their wives, or can be so easily divorced.

Elinor Glyn

Love is just a system for getting someone to call you darling after sex.

Julian Barnes

Men always want to be a woman's first love – women like to be a man's last romance.

Oscar Wilde

I have never met anybody who has been made as happy by love as he has been made sad.

Alice Thomas Ellis

I saw six men kicking and punching the mother-in-law. My neighbor said, "Are you going to help?" I said, "No, six should be enough."

Les Dawson

Love is staying awake all night with a sick child. Or a very healthy adult.

David Frost

Do you seriously expect me to be the first Prince of Wales in history not to have a mistress?

Prince Charles

When my mother-in-law was born, they fired 21 guns. The only trouble was, they all missed.

Les Dawson

My friend spent £50 on a baby alarm and still got pregnant.

Linda Smith

Now the whole dizzying and delirious range of sexual possibilities has been boiled down to that one big, boring, bulimic word *"relationship"*.

Julie Burchill

After eight years with my girlfriend she still gets annoyed if I use her toothbrush. Well, if she can tell me a better way of getting dog shit off my trainers.

Jimmy Carr

Powerful men often succeed through the help of their wives. Powerful women only succeed in spite of their husbands.

Linda Lee-Potter

Changeable women are more endurable than monotonous ones; they are sometimes murdered but rarely deserted.

George Bernard Shaw

My wife said to me, "If you won the lottery, would you still love me?" I said, "Of course I would. I'd miss you, but I'd still love you."

Frank Carson

I hate those ads for air fresheners: they are always populated by women and children, when we all know it is men who make the most smells.

Liz Jones

The war between the sexes is the only one in which both sides regularly sleep with the enemy.

Quentin Crisp

Talk to a woman as if you loved her, and talk to a man as if he bored you.

Oscar Wilde

Men, my dear, are very queer animals – a mixture of horse-nervousness, ass-stubbornness and camel-malice.

Thomas Henry Huxley

British men take you to McDonald's, make you pay and ask if anyone is dating your sister.

Minnie Driver

If I had to choose between him and a cockroach as a companion for a walking tour, the cockroach would have had it by a short head.

P.G. Wodehouse

Mr. Richard Harvey is going to be married, but as it is a great secret and only known to half of the neighborhood, you must not mention it.

Jane Austen

A dentist got married to a manicurist. They fought tooth and nail.

Tommy Cooper

A Royal Engineer serving overseas, wrote 200 love letters a week to his girlfriend back home. This Saturday, at All Saints Church, she marries the postman.

The Weekly Gazette

The only people I care to be very intimate with are the ones you feel would make a good third if God asked you out to dinner.

Nancy Mitford

That's it! I've had enough of men. There isn't one worth shaving your legs for. I'm going back to being a virgin.

Rose, Keeping Up Appearances

At the moment, I am debarred from the pleasure of putting her in her place by the fact that she has not got one.

Edith Sitwell

Love: a mutual misunderstanding

Oscar Wilde

Love is an ocean of emotions entirely surrounded by expenses.

Lord Dewar

⁘

The English really aren't interested in talking to you unless you've been to school or to bed with them.

Lady Nancy Keith

⁘

A man is two people, himself and his cock. A man always takes his friend to the party. Of the two, the friend is the nicer, being more able to show his feelings.

Beryl Bainbridge

⁘

Why are women so much more interesting to men than men are to women?

Virginia Woolf

⁘

I never married because there was no need. I have three pets at home which answer the same purpose as a husband. I have a dog which growls every morning, a parrot which swears all afternoon, and a cat that comes home late at night.

Marie Corelli

⁘

What every woman knows and no man can ever grasp is that even if he brings home everything on the list, he will still not have got the right things.

Allison Pearson

Talk to a man about himself and he will listen for hours.

Benjamin Disraeli

No one listened to one unless one said the wrong thing.

Sylvia Townsend Warner

We were married for better or worse. I couldn't have done better, and she couldn't have done worse.

Henny Youngman

When a man brings his wife flowers for no reason, there's a reason.

Molly McGee

A true friend stabs you in the front.

Oscar Wilde

It's a dilemma to not only have to choose what outfit to wear but which boyfriend to wear it with.

Tara Palmer-Tomkinson

It goes far towards reconciling me to being a woman when I reflect that I am thus in no danger of marrying one.

Lady Mary Wortley Montagu

She sat listening to the speech with the stoical indifference with which an Eskimo might accept the occurrence of a snowstorm the more, in the course of an Arctic winter.

Saki

Women, without her man, is nothing.

Women: without her, man is nothing.

Statement showing the importance of punctuation

There is only one thing in the world worse than being talked about, and that is not being talked about.

Oscar Wilde

Gossip is when you hear something you like about someone you don't.

Jane Seabrook

We always hold hands. If I let go, she shops.

Henny Youngman

I never knew how exciting dating could be until I got married.

Melanie White

Love is sharing your popcorn.

Charles Schultz

Love; A temporary insanity curable by marriage.

Ambrose Bierce

As a man in a relationship, you have a choice: You can be right or you can be happy.

Ralphie May

What's the best way to have your husband remember your anniversary? Get married on his birthday.

Cindy Garner

An archaeologist is the best husband any woman can have; the older she gets, the more interested he is in her.

Agatha Christie

Whatever you may look like, marry a man your own age - as your beauty fades, so will his eyesight.

Phyllis Diller

Spend a few minutes a day really listening to your spouse. No matter how stupid his problems sound to you.

Megan Mullally

Marrying a man is like buying something you've been admiring for a long time in a shop window. You may love it when you get it home, but it doesn't always go with everything else.

Jean Kerr

The secret of a happy marriage remains a secret.

Henny Youngman

A successful relationship requires falling in love many times, always with the same person.

Mignon McLaughlin

Gravitation is not responsible for people falling in love.

Albert Einstein

Men are far more romantic than women. Men are the ones who'll say, "I've found somebody. She's amazing. If I don't get to be with this person, I can't carry on. If I'm not with her I'll end up in a bedsit, I'll be an alcoholic." That's how women feel about shoes.

Dylan Moran

Why buy a book when you can join the library?

Lily Savage, on marriage

❧

I never feel more alone than when I'm trying to put sunscreen on my back.

Jimmy Kimmel

❧

Instead of getting married again, I'm going to find a woman I don't like and just give her a house.

Rod Stewart, rock star

❧

I think it should be like dog licenses. I think you should have to renew your marriage licenses every five years.

John Cleese

❧

Marriage is a sort of friendship recognized by the police.

Robert Louis Stevenson

❧

FRIENDSHIP

Friendship is not possible between two women, one of whom is very well dressed.

Laurie Colwin

There is nothing better than a friend unless it is a friend with chocolate.

Linda Grayson

One sure way to lose another woman's friendship is to try to improve her flower arrangements.

Marcelene Cox

A good friend will help you move. But a best friend will help you move a dead body.

Jim Hayes

A friend is someone who knows all about you and still loves you.

Elbert Hubbard

When you're in jail, a good friend will be trying to bail you out. A best friend will be in the cell next to you saying, Damn, that was fun.

Groucho Marx

Some people go to priests; others to poetry; I to my friends.

Virginia Woolf

Most of us don't need a psychiatric therapist as much as a friend to be silly with.

Robert Brault

Men kick friendship around like a football and it doesn't seem to crack. Women treat it like glass and it falls to pieces.

Anne Lindbergh

The holy passion of friendship is so sweet and steady and loyal and enduring a nature that it will last through a whole lifetime, if not asked to lend money.

Mark Twain

CHILDREN

The main purpose of children's parties is to remind you that there are children more awful than your own.

Katherine Whitehorn

When your children are teenagers, it's important to have a dog so that someone in the house is happy to see you.

Nora Ephron

I'm very hairy on my body and my wife is very ginger. We could very easily have an orang-utan.

Mike Gunn

Cleaning up with children around is like shoveling during a blizzard.

Margaret Culkin Banning

Children

Before I got married, I had six theories about bringing up children; now I have six children and no theories.

John Wilmot

❧

We spend the first twelve months of our children's lives teaching them to walk and talk and the next twelve telling them to sit down and shut up.

Phyllis Diller

❧

Sometimes I am amazed that my wife and I created two human beings from scratch yet struggle to assemble the most basic of IKEA cabinets.

Malcolm Prince

❧

They say men can never experience the pain of childbirth. They can if you hit them in the goolies with a cricket bat for fourteen hours.

Jo Brand

❧

Adults are just children who earn money.

Kenneth Branagh

❧

I asked my brother-in-law, the father of four boys, 'If you had it to do all over again, would you still have kids?' 'Yes,' he said. 'Just not these four.'

Sheila Lee

I once bought my kids a set of batteries for Christmas with a note on it, saying, "Toys not included".

Bernard Manning

Youth is such a wonderful thing. What a crime to waste it on children.

George Bernard Shaw

A lot of mothers will do anything for their children, except let them be themselves.

Banksy

I'd like to smack smug parents who say, "Our three-year-old's reading *Harry Potter*." Well, my three-year-old's smearing his shit on the fridge door.

Jack Dee

Children

I really think that girls are born in conversation. I think they just pop out of the womb going, "Are you my mother? Lovely to put a name to a face. You, nurse, weigh me. Get it over with; it's the best it's ever going to be. Seven pounds one? It's downhill from here.

Michael McIntyre

When childhood dies, its corpses are called adults.

Brian Aldiss

Parents should leave books lying around marked "Forbidden" if they want their children to read.

Doris Lessing

If men had to have babies, they would only ever have one each.

Princess Diana

I don't dislike babies, though I think very young ones rather disgusting.

Queen Victoria

We have lots of rows about the whole baby thing. I wanted to have a baby for about five years, but my wife wants to keep it forever.

Lee Mack

Bringing up children on your own is very difficult, even when there are two parents.

Virginia Bottomley

Insanity is hereditary – you get it from your children.

Sam Levenson

Children

Sex

I wouldn't kidnap a man for sex, but I'm not saying I couldn't use someone to oil the mower.

Victoria Wood

Yesterday morning my wife asked me to make love to her in the kitchen. When I asked why, she said the egg timer had broken and she wanted a soft-boiled egg.

David Brinham

When the sun comes up, I have morals again.

Elizabeth Taylor

I don't find English men sexy. They're all queer or kinky. The last Pom I went to bed with said to me, "Let's pretend you're dead."

Germaine Greer

Susan, you are offering this man food and sex in the same place. If there's something to read in the loo he may never leave.

Sally Harper (Kate Isitt), Coupling

❧

People today say you cannot be happy unless your sex life is happy. That makes about as much sense as saying you cannot be happy unless your golf life is happy.

Evelyn Waugh

❧

I had a wet dream about you last night. I dreamed you got hit by a bus, and I pissed myself laughing.

Jack Dee

❧

The total amount of undesired sex endured by women is probably greater in marriage than in prostitution.

Bertrand Russell

❧

I said to my wife, "Was you faking it last night?" She said, "No, I really was asleep."

Ricky Grover

❧

It's incredible what men will interpret as sexual: "Did you see the way she looked at me before she told me to fuck off?"

Dylan Moran

When I had my daughters, I had to have stitches. I did ask them to put a couple of extra ones in, as a special treat for me husband, really. He said it really improved things. He said before that it was like waving a stick in the Albert Hall.

Pauline Calf (a.k.a Steve Coogan)

Sex is like supermarkets – overrated. Just a lot of pushing and shoving and you still come out with very little at the end.

Shirley Valentine

Why should we take advice on sex from the Pope? If he knows anything about it, he shouldn't.

George Bernard Shaw

Sex, on the whole, was meant to be short, nasty and brutish. If what you want is cuddling, you should buy a puppy.

Julie Burchill

Sex

Sex was not a subject we discussed in our family. I didn't even realize I had a vagina. The loss of my virginity was a process so lengthy and so painful that I thought, Oh, I see, the man actually has to make the hole by pounding away with his penis.

Julie Walters

I've only slept with men I've been married to. How many women can make that claim?

Elizabeth Taylor

Ken is so tired his sperm are on crutches.

Emma Thompson, on ex-husband Kenneth Branagh

I've never ever had sex apart from that one time eight months ago but apart from that I'm a complete virgin.

Vicky Pollard, Little Britain

At the Army medical, the doctor said, "Take all your clothes off." I said, "Shouldn't you take me out to dinner first?"

Spike Milligan

It's an extraordinary way of bringing babies into the world. I don't know how God thought of it

Winston Churchill

Who is this Greek chap Clitoris they're talking about?

Lord Albermarle

My wife is a sex object – every time I ask for sex, she objects.

Les Dawson

Sex

SPORT

If you want to understand the effect of weight on a horse, try running for a bus with nothing in your hands. Then try doing it with your hands full of shopping. Then think about doing that for four and a half miles.

Jenny Pitman

Have you ever thought about the person who designed the sports skirt? Somebody sat down, drew a fantasy and made it compulsory uniform. I can never watch Wimbledon without thinking of that man.

Inspector Morse

When male golfers wiggle their feet to get their stance right, they look exactly like cats preparing to pee.

Jilly Cooper

- How do you think golf could be improved?

- I always feel that the hole is too small.

Interviewer with Mark James

I don't know much about football. I know what a goal is, which is surely the main thing about football.

Victoria Beckham

Fashion & Beauty

The sense of being well-dressed gives a feeling of inward tranquility, which religion is powerless to bestow.

C.F. Forbes

How on earth did Gandhi manage to walk so far in flip-flops? I can't last ten minutes in mine.

Mrs. Merton

After forty, a woman has to choose between losing her figure or her face. My advice is to keep your face and stay sitting down.

Dame Barbara Cartland

She wore far too much rouge last night and not quite enough clothes. That is always a sign of despair in a woman.

Oscar Wilde

Beauty is the first present nature gives to a woman and the first it takes away.

Fay Weldon

Nothing inspires cleanliness more than an unexpected guest.

Radhika Mundra

I can never be a nudist. I could never decide what not to wear.

Jennifer Coombs

They say leather is mainly for perverts. Don't know why. Think it's very practical, actually. I mean, you spill anything on it, and it just comes of. I suppose that could be why the perverts like it.

Charlotte Coleman

One thing I've learned from Star Trek is that men are going to be wearing simple pullovers forever. I've also learned, not to my surprise, that women will continue to sport minis and plenty of décolletages whatever the stardate.

Bernard Hollowood

The best-dressed woman is one whose clothes wouldn't look too strange in the country.

Hardy Amies

There is no cosmetic for beauty like happiness.

Lady Blessington

There is no cosmetic for beauty like happiness.

I love new clothes. If everyone could just wear new clothes every day, I reckon depression wouldn't exist anymore.

Sophie Kinsella

Nothing gives a brighter glow to the complexion or makes the eye of a beautiful woman sparkle so intensely as triumph over another.

Lady Caroline Lamb

- I'm lending Nancy Mitford my villa in France so she can finish a book.

- Oh, really. What's she reading?

Friend and Dame Edith Evans

I dress sexily – but not in an obvious way; sexy in a virginal way.

Victoria Beckham

It has been said that a pretty face is a passport. But it's not, it's a visa, and it runs out fast.

Julie Burchill

The problem with beauty is that it's like being born rich and getting poorer.

Joan Collins

I have a suspicion that the photos on seed packets are posed by professional flowers.

Denis Norden

Do you know a shop where they cut your hair properly? I keep on having my hair cut, but it keeps on growing again.

G. K. Chesterton

Let us be grateful to the mirror for revealing to us our appearance only.

Samuel Butler

Well, madam, have you looked in the mirror and seen the state of your nose? Boxing is my excuse. What's yours?

Henry Cooper to Baroness Summerskill

The reason there are so few female politicians is that it is too much trouble to put make-up on two faces.

Maureen Murphy

I lent my wife £1,000 to have for plastic surgery; now I can't get the money back and I don't know who to look for.

Jethro (a.k.a. Geoff Rowe)

I wish I was covered in fur . . . or feathers . . . or something more interesting than just fat.

John Peel

Fashion is a form of ugliness so intolerable that we have to alter it every six months.

Oscar Wilde

The buttocks are the most aesthetically pleasing part of the body because they are non-functional. Although they conceal an essential orifice, these pointless globes are as near as the human form can ever come to abstract art.

Kenneth Tynan

My face is like five miles of bad country road.

Richard Harris

ART & CULTURE

All this modern art looks like bollocks so it must be worth something.

Edina Monsoon

All this modern art looks like bollocks so it must be worth something.

Frankenstein is a book about what happens when a man tries to have a baby without a woman.

Anne K. Mellor

 The difference between fiction and reality? Fiction has to make sense.

Tom Clancy, author

You should always believe what you read in newspapers, for that makes them more interesting.

Rose Macaulay

I told my mother I wanted to grow up and be a comedian. She said you can't do both.

Jimmy Carr

No good opera plot can be sensible, for people do not sing when they are feeling sensible.

W.H. Auden

An ambulance chasing a fire engine round a roundabout.

Dylan Moran, on dance music

All you have to do is to look like crap on film, and everyone thinks you're a brilliant actress. Actually, all you've done is look like crap.

Helen Mirren

My dad said, "Laughter is the best medicine," which is why, when I was six, I nearly died of diphtheria: "Dad, I can't breathe!" "Knock, knock . . ."

Dave Spikey

Television is for appearing on, not looking at.

Noel Coward

She has the smile of a woman who has just dined off her husband.

Lawrence Durrell, on the Mona Lisa

Every portrait that is painted with feeling is a portrait of the artist, not of the sitter.

Oscar Wilde

Ladies, just a little more virginity, if you don't mind.

Herbert Beertbohm Tree

The sound of laughter is the most civilized music in the world.

Peter Ustinov

Orlando Bloom sounds like the love-child of Virginia Woolf and James Joyce.

Quentin Cooper

Television is as injurious to the soul as fast food is to the body.

Quentin Crisp

A bad experience of Shakespeare is like a bad oyster – it puts you off for life.

Judi Dench

The length of a film should be directly related to the endurance of the human bladder.

Alfred Hitchcock

I love acting. It is so much more real than life.

Oscar Wilde

Bach almost persuades me to be a Christian.

Virginia Woolf

Bells are music's laughter.

Thomas Hood

They say an actor is only as good as his parts. Well, my parts have done me pretty well, darling.

Barbara Windsor

Sometimes people confuse me with Anthony Hopkins. Here's how you tell the difference: I'm the one nailing Mrs. Hopkins.

Michael Caine

If Peter O'Toole were any prettier, you'd have to call the film *Florence of Arabia.*

Noel Coward

Sometimes an orgasm is better than being on the stage. Sometimes being on the stage is better than an orgasm.

Mick Jagger

Comedy is the one job you can do badly and no one will laugh at you.

Max Miller

Two people writing a novel is like three people having a baby.

Evelyn Waugh

The finest collection of frames I ever saw.

Sir Humphry Davy on the Paris art galleries

Agatha Christie has given more pleasure in bed than any other woman.

Nancy Banks-Smith

- Two tickets reserved for you for the first night of my new play. Bring a friend. If you have one.

- Cannot make the first night. Will come the second night. If you have one.

George Bernard Shaw and Winston Churchill

There are two motives for reading a book: one, that you enjoy it; the other, that you can boast about it.

Bertrand Russell

Literature is the art of writing something that will be read twice; journalism what will be grasped at once.

Cyril Connolly

HOBBIES & FUN

Recreation: hunting, fishing, shooting, food, rugby, men.

Clarissa Dickson Wright

The British are not good at having fun. I get overexcited if there's a pattern on my kitchen roll.

Victoria Wood

You can't get a cup of tea big enough or a book long enough to suit me.

C.S. Lewis

You know what really pisses me off? When you're on a plane, and the hostess comes up to you and asks you to stop singing. Hold on, you've been giving me free drinks for five hours – what do you expect me to do?

Sean Lock

For men, shopping is like sex. They can only manage it for five minutes and then they get tired.

Jeff Green

I went window shopping today. I bought four windows.

Tommy Cooper

At the age of 80, there are very few pleasures left to me, but one of them is passive smoking.

Baroness Trumpington

One half of the world cannot understand the pleasure of the other.

Jane Austen

To truly laugh, you must be able to take your pain, and play with it.

Charlie Chaplin

Happiness is the perpetual possession of being well deceived.

Lytton Strachey

Some cause happiness wherever they go; others, whenever they go.

Oscar Wilde

The only way of preventing civilized men from beating and kicking their wives is to organize games in which they can kick and beat balls.

George Bernard Shaw

Let's face it; football is a game of the commoners. As soon as you get a mortgage, you start liking tennis.

Jonathan Ross

Bad humor is an evasion of reality; good humor is an acceptance of it.

Malcolm Muggeridge

To relax, I put Smarties tubes on cats' legs to make them walk like a robot. If I'm really in the mood for fun, I make them walk downstairs.

Jimmy Carr

Imagination was given to man to compensate him for what he is not, a sense of humor to console him for what he is.

Francis Bacon, philosopher

I remember once having to stop performing when I thought an elderly man a few rows back from the front was actually going to die because he was laughing so hard.

Adrian Edmondson

In 1969 I gave up drinking and sex. It was the worst twenty minutes of my life.

George Best

- So, you got drunk again last night. Why was that?

- Because I was sober.

Ardal O'Hanlon

KNOWLEDGE & EDUCATION

Lack of education is an extraordinary handicap when one is being offensive.

Josephine Tay

The first time you leave your child at school you're faced with a tough decision – down the pub or back to bed?

Jo Brand

I spend all my time arguing with the spell-check on my computer.

Ann Widdecombe

He is the intellectual without the intellect.

John McKenna

I chose a single-sex Oxford college because I thought I'd rather not face the trauma of men at breakfast.

Theresa May

I am patient with stupidity but not with those who are proud of it.

Edith Sitwell

The greatest life lesson is to know that even fools are sometimes right.

Winston Churchill

Originality is undetected plagiarism.

Dean Inge

Nothing that is worth knowing could be taught.

Oscar Wilde

To know all is not to forgive all. It is to despise everybody.

Quentin Crisp

I'd always thought her half-baked, but now I think they didn't even put her in the oven.

P.G. Wodehouse

A great many of people think they are thinking when they are merely rearranging their prejudices.

William James

If there was graffiti in a lavatory cubicle, I had to read every word and sometimes even corrected the spelling and punctuation.

Sue Townsend

This is the sort of English up with which I will not put.

Winston Churchill

The trouble with words is that you never know· whose mouth they've been in.

Dennis Potter

The only time my education was interrupted was when I was at school.

George Bernard Shaw

Men are born ignorant, not stupid. They are made stupid by education.

Bertrand Russell

My school report said that I was every inch a fool. Fortunately, I was not very tall.

Sir Norman Wisdom

LUCK & HAPPINESS

The British do not expect happiness. I had the impression, all the time that I lived there, that they did not want to be happy; they want to be right.

Quentin Crisp

A large income is the best recipe for happiness I ever heard of.

Jane Austen

The insurance man told me that the accident policy covered falling off the roof but not hitting the ground.

Tommy Cooper

If you want to be happy for a short time, get drunk; happy for a long time, fall in love; happy forever, take up gardening.

Arthur Smith

All the things I like to do are either immoral, illegal, or fattening.

Alexander Woollcott, actor

Good friends, good books, and a sleepy conscience: this is the ideal life.

Mark Twain

A short message from the Editor

Hey, hope you're enjoying the book. I'd love to hear your thoughts!

Many readers do not know how hard reviews are to come by, and how much they help an author.

I would be incredibly thankful if you could take just 60 seconds to write a brief review on Amazon, even if it's just a few sentences!

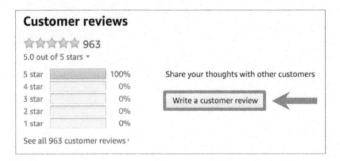

Please scan the QR code below to leave your review:

Thank you for taking the time to share your thoughts!

Your review will genuinely make a difference for me and help gain exposure for my work.

FOOD & DRINK

English coffee tastes the way a long-standing family joke sounds when you try to explain it to outsiders.

Margaret Halsey

If you want to confuse a girl, buy her a pair of chocolate shoes.

Milton Jones

Pratchett's guide to mushrooms: One: All fungi are edible. Two: Some fungi are not edible more than once.

Terry Pratchett

Never drink black coffee at lunch; it will keep you awake all afternoon.

Jilly Cooper

Triangular sandwiches taste better than square ones.

Peter Kay

❧

Stop being a vegan and start enjoying what you eat.

Jamie Oliver

❧

They say cheese gives you nightmares. Ridiculous! I'm not scared of cheese!

Ross Noble

❧

Why does mineral water that "has trickled through mountains for centuries" have a "use-by" date?

Peter Kay

❧

If the British can survive their meals, they can survive anything.

George Bernard Shaw

❧

CHARACTER & MANNERS

Even crushed against his brother in the Tube, the average Englishman pretends desperately that he is alone.

Germaine Greer

Manners are especially the need of the plain. The pretty can get away with anything.

Evelyn Waugh

Depression is the most extreme form of vanity.

Julie Burchill

My kids have beautiful manners. Our Jason may be a car thief, but he always leaves a thank-you note on the pavement.

Lily Savage

She never lets ideas interrupt the easy flow of her conversation.

Jean Webster, author

- I will not fuck it up again, Mum.

- Bridget! Language!

- Sorry. I will not fuck it up again, Mother.

Bridget Jones and Mum, Bridget Jones – The Edge of Reason

I am all in favor of spontaneity, providing it is carefully planned and ruthlessly controlled.

John Gielgud

If there's one thing I can't stand it's snobbism. People who pretend they're superior make it so much harder for those of us who really are.

Haycinth Bucket, Keeping Up Appearances

He ought to run a hospital for sick jokes.

Anthony Powell

Angels can fly because they take things lightly.

G. K. Chesterton

Last time I went on an Intercity train there were a couple across the aisle having sex. Of course, this being a British train, nobody said anything. Then they finished, they both lit up a cigarette and this woman stood up and said, "Excuse me, I think you'll find this is a non-smoking compartment."

Victoria Wood

Be wiser than other people, if you can, but do not tell them so.

Lord Chesterfield

It seldom pays to be rude. It never pays to be half-rude.

Norman Douglas

A gentleman is one who can fold a newspaper in a crowded train.

Leonora Cunningham

Silence is the correct answer to an unasked question.

Armando Iannucci

My wife loves the c-word. Sometimes, when the children are listening, she combines it with "bastard" to create "custard".

Jeremy Clarkson

❦

The mechanic said that if it had been a horse, he'd have had to shoot her.

Basil Boothroyd

❦

After a taxi ride, Tommy Cooper would slip something into the top pocket of the driver and say, "Have a drink on me." When the taxi driver looked in his pocket, he'd find it was a teabag.

Bob Monkhouse

❦

Could you ask our captain to go a little faster and land a little earlier? My husband would tip him handsomely.

Hyacinth Bucket, at the check-in desk, Keeping Up Appearances

❦

I looked up some of the symptoms of pregnancy: moody, irritable, big bosoms. I've obviously been pregnant for 36 years.

Victoria Wood

❦

I believe in the discipline of silence and could talk for hours about it.

George Bernard Shaw

If you apologize for turning your back, the Chinese reply, "A rose has no back."

Geoffrey Madan

A little nonsense now and then is cherished by the wisest men.

Roald Dahl

If you believe that your thoughts originate inside your brain, do you also believe that television shows are made inside your television set?

Warren Ellis

I still like a man to open a door for me – even if he does let it swing back and hit me in the face.

Pauline Daniels

I love children – especially when they cry, for then someone takes them away.

Nancy Mitford

My New Year's resolution is to refrain from saying witty, unkind things unless they are really witty and irreparably damaging.

James Agate

Intuition is the strange instinct that tells a woman she is right, whether she is or not.

Oscar Wilde

During an outing on a safari trip to Africa with a group of fellow British tourists, a friend of mine stopped for a pee. Having located a suitable bush, she relieved herself but was amazed at standing up to find a queue of ladies behind her all waiting for the same bush.

Catherine Betts

This is the only country in the world where you step on somebody's foot, and he apologizes.

Keith Waterhous on England

If you can't be a good example, then you'll just have to serve as a horrible warning.

Catherine Aird

A man who moralizes is usually a hypocrite, and a woman who moralizes is invariably plain.

Oscar Wilde

The lie is the basic building block of good manners. That may seem mildly shocking to a moralist – but then what isn't?

Quentin Crisp

His courtesy was somewhat extravagant. He would write and thank the people who wrote to thank him for wedding presents, and when he encountered anyone as punctilious as himself, the correspondence ended only with death.

Evelyn Waugh

First things first, but not necessarily in that order.

Dr. Who

Ghosts, like ladies, never speak till spoke to.

Richard Harris Braham

I could not fail to disagree with you less.

Boris Johnson

There are some people who suddenly get loads of money who become very tasteless. How have you two managed to avoid that?

Ali G (a.k.a. Sacha Baron Cohen), interviewing David and Victoria Beckham for Comic Relief

Manners are the outward expression of expert interior decoration.

Noel Coward

My father and he had one of those English friendships which begin by avoiding intimacies and eventually eliminate speech altogether.

Jorge Luis Borges

The English never speak to anyone unless they have been properly introduced (except in case of shipwreck).

Pierre Daninos

A gentleman never eats. He breakfasts, he lunches, he dines, but he never eats.

Lord Fotherham

The more the English dislike you, the more polite they are.

Rabbi Lionel Blue

CLASS & ROYALTY

Middle-class girls get degrees. The working class get jobs. And the underclass get a baby as soon as they can.

Tony Parsons

It was lovely to talk to the Queen, especially since I am a Windsor too.

Barbara Windsor

Never keep up with the Joneses. Drag them down to your level. It's cheaper.

Quentin Crisp

Oh, I do hope you're not going to spoil everything with lower-middle-class humor.

Hyacinth Bucket, Keeping Up Appearances

Prince Andrew and Sarah met on the polo field, doesn't everybody?

Susan Barrantes, mother of Sarah Fergusen

Buckingham Palace rejected a suggestion by Mrs. Thatcher that a procedure be instituted to ensure she and the Queen never appear in public in similar or identical outfits with this terse reply: "Her Majesty never notices what anyone wears."

Laura Grey

Isn't it amazing that Camilla looks exactly like Princess Diana if she had survived the car crash?

Frankie Boyle

How low and unbecoming a thing laughing is: not to mention the disagreeable noise that it makes and the shocking distortion of the face.

Lord Chesterfield

The trouble with being a princess is that it's so hard to have a pee.

Princess Diana

The post is hopeless, and I have given up sending things by post. I have things delivered in my Rolls Royce.

Barbara Cartland

How shall we ever know if it's morning if there's no servant to pull up the blind?

J.M. Barrie, The Admirable Crichton

Gentlemen are requested, and servants are commanded to keep off the grass.

Sign in London park, 19th century

"How wonderful it must have been for the Ancient Britons," my mother said once, "when the Romans arrived, and they could have a Hot Bath."

Katharine Whitehorn

HEALTH

- How are you feeling?

- I'm dying but otherwise, I'm in perfect health.

Friend and Edith Sitwell

When I was a nurse, my favorite assignment was the anorexic ward. Sometimes I ate as many as 17 dinners.

Jo Brand

Lord Dawson was not a good doctor. King George V told me that he would not have died, had he had another doctor.

Margot Asquith

Be careful about reading health books. You may die of a misprint.

Mark Twain

Free your mind, and your bottom will follow.

Sarah Ferguson

꧁꧂

I've got my figure back after giving birth. Sad, I'd hope to get somebody else's.

Caroline Quentin

꧁꧂

I asked my doctor for something for persistent wind. He gave me a kite.

Les Dawson

꧁꧂

Wine; a constant proof that God loves us and loves to see us happy.

Benjamin Franklin

꧁꧂

FOOD & DIET

I would walk miles for a bacon sandwich.

Diana, Princess of Wales

I'm in shape. Round is a shape.

George Carlin

Don't dig your grave with your knife and fork.

English proverb.

Things taste better in small houses.

Queen Victoria

I found out there was only one way to look thin: hang out with fat people.

Rodney Dangerfield

I love the philosophy of a sandwich. It typifies my attitude to life. It's all there, it's fun, it looks good, and you don't have to wash up afterwards.

Molly Parkin

A woman should never be seen eating or drinking, unless it be lobster, salad and champagne, the only truly feminine viands.

Lord Byron

Tourists tend to enjoy the traditional English breakfast because they don't eat such things often at home. If they did, they would die.

Lonely Planet guide to Britain

Diets are like boyfriends – it never really works to go back to them.

Nigella Lawson

The name Big Mac is generally supposed to have come about because it is a big McDonald's burger, but in fact, it was named after a big raincoat whose taste resembles.

Joe Brand

The Englishman who visits Mount Etna will carry his tea kettle to the top.

Ralph Waldo Emerson

I just love Chinese food. My favorite dish is number twenty-seven.

Clement Attlee

ANIMALS

I dislike monkeys: they always remind me of my poor relations.

Henry Lutrell

A dog is not intelligent. Never trust an animal that's surprised by its own farts.

Frank Skinner

Why didn't evolution give them genes to make them good at carpentry, then, so they could build a ladder instead of growing long necks?

Karl Pilkington, on giraffes

If God did not intend for us to eat animals, then why did he make them out of meat?

John Cleese

A dog teaches a boy fidelity, perseverance, and to turn around three times before lying down.

Robert Benchley, humorist

A man loses his dog so he puts an ad in the paper. And the ad says, "Here boy!"

Spike Milligan

Cats are smarter than dogs. You can't get eight cats to pull a sled through snow.

Jeff Valdez, producer

Did St. Francis preach to the birds? Whatever for? If he really liked birds, he would have done better to preach the cats.

Rebecca West

A bird in the hand invariably shits on your wrist.

Billy Connolly

Red squirrels . . . you don't see many of them since they became extinct.

Michael Aspel

Why do dogs always race to the door when the doorbell rings when it's hardly ever for them?

Harry Hill

The male gypsy moth can smell the female gypsy moth up to seven miles away – and that fact also works if you remove the word "moth".

Jimmy Carr

Dogs look up to you. Cats look down to you. Give me a pig. He just looks you in the eye and treats you as an equal.

Winston Churchill

Among the mammals, only man has ears that can display no emotion.

W. H. Auden

If you leave a dog locked in a car on a hot day, it will die in about half an hour. If you leave the heating on, you can get that down to about ten minutes.

Sean Meo

LIFE & DEATH

Life was planned by a committee while the clever ones had popped
out to the lav.

Victoria Wood

If you don't know where you are going, any road will get you there.

Lewis Carroll

Men were born to lie, and women to believe them.

John Gay

Life's not fair, is it? Some of us drink champagne in the fast lane,
and some of us eat our sandwiches by the loose chippings on the
A597.

Victoria Wood

I have a nervous breakdown in the film, and in one scene, I get to stand at the top of the stairs waving an empty sherry bottle which is, of course, a typical scene from my daily life, so isn't much of a stretch.

Emma Thompson

I was taking my dog for a stroll in the cemetery early one day, and a woman passed me by and said, "Morning!" I said, "No, just walking the dog."

John Mann

If you live to be one hundred, you've got it made. Very few people die past that age.

George Burns

In Liverpool, the difference between a funeral and a wedding is one less drunk.

Paul O'Grady

The leading cause of death in this world is birth.

Mitch Murray

I wouldn't say my mother-in-law is fat, but when she was run over recently the driver said it was because he didn't have enough petrol to go around her.

Jimmy Tarbuck

- So. You're going to Parslow's funeral.

- Yes. Even though it's very unlikely that he'll ever come to mine.

Mrs. Blewitt and Arkwright, Open All Hours

I'm fascinated that hair grows after death; I'm looking forward to that.

Clive Anderson

I'm looking forward to

Death is the last enemy: once we've got past that, I think everything will be all right.

Alice Thomas Ellis

Have you noticed that all the people in favor of birth control are already born?

Benny Hill

It's a good rule of life never to apologize. The right sort of people don't want apologies, and the wrong sort takes a mean advantage of them.

P. G. Wodehouse

Remember, if a man twists his wife, he will twist anyone else.

Norris McWhirter

Parents are the bones on which children sharpen their teeth.

Peter Ustinov

I don't know what I want, but I want it NOW!

Vivian Stanshall

For sale: Undertaker's overcoat. Slightly worn on one shoulder.

Loot Magazine

I blame myself for my boyfriend's death. I shot him.

Jo Brand

After being an awed witness of the funeral of King Edward VII, the little daughter of Lord Kinnoull refused to say her prayers that night: "God will be too busy unpacking King Edward," she said.

Lord Riddell

Well, thank you, Rector, it was a lovely funeral. We must have one again sometime.

Audrey Ffrobes-Hamilton, To The Manor Born

Should a father be present at the birth of his child? It's all any reasonable child can expect if dad is present at the conception.

Joe Orton

We cannot tear out a single page of our life, but we can throw the whole book in the fire.

George Eliot

I hope I go like my mother. She just sat up, broke wind, and died.

Ena Sharples, Coronation Street

The trouble with children is that they are not returnable.

Quentin Crisp

A French five minutes is ten minutes shorter than a Spanish five minutes but slightly longer than an English five minutes, which is usually ten minutes.

Guy Bellamy

For most people, death comes at the end of their lives.

Greater London radio presenter

Everyone seems to fear dying alone, and I have never understood this point of view. Who wants to have to die and be polite at the same time?

Quentin Crisp

Life is a tragedy when seen in close-up, but a comedy in long-shot.

Charlie Chaplin

When you've told someone that you've left them a legacy, the only decent thing to do is to die at once.

Samuel Butler

Dear World, I am leaving because I am bored. I feel I have lived long enough. I am leaving you with your worries in this sweet cesspool. Good luck.

George Sanders, Suicide note

There are many who dare not kill themselves for fear of what the neighbors will say.

Cyril Connolly

You live and learn. Then you die and forget it all.

Noel Coward

May you die in bed at 95, shot by a jealous spouse.

Irish blessing

While other people's deaths are deeply sad, one's own is surely a bit of a joke.

James Cameron

⁘

Crucifixion… it's a slow, horrible death. But at least it gets you out into the open.

Matthias, Monty Python's Life of Brian

⁘

I never made a mistake in my life. I thought I did once, but I was wrong.

Charles M. Schulz

⁘

Life is hard; it's harder if you're stupid.

John Wayne

⁘

Life is like a roll of toilet paper, hopefully long and useful, but it always ends at the wrong moment.

Rudyh

⁘

My life has no purpose, no direction, no aim, no meaning, and yet I'm happy. I can't figure it out. What am I doing right?

Charles Schulz

Life is funny; when you are young, you want to be older, and those that are older wish to be younger.

Karon Waddell

Life is so constructed that an event does not, cannot, will not, match the expectation.

Charlotte Bronte

Life does not cease to be funny when people die any more than it ceases to be serious when people laugh.

George Bernard Shaw

Life is hard, after all, it kills you.

Kathrine Hepburn

We all pay for life with death, so everything in between should be free.

Bill Hicks

Embrace the glorious mess that you are.

Elizabeth Gilbert

Don't worry about the world coming to an end today. It's already tomorrow in Australia.

Charles M. Schulz

CRIME & PUNISHMENT

If you are ever attacked in the street, do not shout "Help!", shout "Fire!". People adore fires and always come rushing. Nobody will come if you shout "Help!".

Jean Trumpington

Sentence first, verdict afterwards.

Lewis Carroll, Alice's Adventures in Wonderland

Justice is being allowed to do whatever I like. Injustice is whatever prevents me doing it.

Samuel Butler

Crime is terribly revealing. Try and vary your methods as you will, your tastes, your habits, your attitude of mind, and your soul is revealed by your actions.

Agatha Christie

"Senseless" is a word usually applied to vandalism, but when one grasps the simple proposition that vandals obviously enjoy breaking things, the vandalism is no more senseless than playing tennis.

Auberon Waugh

Ma always told me she used to keep half a brick in her handbag, just in case.

Michael Bentine

A lawyer will do anything to win a case; sometimes, he will even tell the truth.

Patrick Murray

There is no satisfaction in hanging a man who does not object to it.

George Bernard Shaw

One wonders what would happen in a society in which there were no rules to break. Doubtless, everyone would quickly die of boredom.

Susan Howatch

AGE

People always live forever when there is any annuity to be paid to them.

Jane Austen

Middle age is when you look at the rain teeming down and say: "That'll be good for the garden."

Grace Marshall

The secret to staying young is to live honestly, eat slowly, and lie about your age.

Lucille Ball

Moisturizers do work. The rest is pap. There is nothing on God's earth that will take away 30 years of arguing with your husband.

Anita Roddick

Age is an issue of mind over matter. If you don't mind, it doesn't matter.

Mark Twain

How long a minute is, depends on which side of the bathroom door you're in.

Rob Monkhouse

I've found a way to make my wife drive more carefully. I told her that if she has an accident, the newspapers would print her age.

Jim Murray

A man's as old as he's feeling. A woman is as old as she looks.

Samuel Taylor Coleridge

As you get older, three things happen. The first is your memory goes, and I can't remember the other two . . .

Norman Wisdom

The old believe everything, the middle-aged suspect everything, the young know everything.

Oscar Wilde

There are three classes into which all the women past seventy that ever I knew were to be divided. One: That dear old soul; two: That old woman; three: That old witch.

Samuel Taylor Coleridge

Age

RELIGION

I asked him why he was a priest, and he said if you have to work for anybody, an absentee boss is best.

Jeanette Winterson

I'm not a religious woman, but I find if you say no to everything, you can hardly tell the difference.

Mrs. Featherstone, Open All Hours

When I was in a convent in Belgium, I had to bathe in a bath which was sheeted over to prevent my guardian angel from seeing me.

Marie Tempest

The first time I sang in the church choir, two hundred people changed their religion.

Fred Allen

If Jesus was a Jew, how come he has a Mexican first name?

Billy Connolly

We were discussing the possibility of making one of our cats Pope recently, and we decided that the fact that she was not Italian, and she was female, made the third point, that she was a cat, quite irrelevant.

Katherine Whitehorn

My heaven will be filled with wonderful young men and dukes.

Barbara Cartland

One thing I shall miss in heaven is gardening. We shan't have weeds in heaven, shall we?

Catherine Bramwell-Booth

Two guys came knocking at my door once and said, "We want to talk to you about Jesus." I said, "Oh, no, what's he done now?"

Kevin McAleer

We know he [Jesus Christ] wasn't English because he wore sandals, but never with socks.

Linda Smith

My mother was worried about whether my father would be wearing pajamas or mackintosh in the afterlife.

George Melly

Prayers must not be answered: if it is, it ceases to be prayers and becomes correspondence.

Oscar Wilde

In the Bible: No one coughs. One person sneezes. Only one woman's age is mentioned (Sarah: 127).

Geoffrey Madan

Historically, more people have died of religion than of cancer.

Dick Francis

When I was a child, I used to think that the Day of Judgement meant that we were all going to judge God, and I still don't see why not.

Lord Berners

Men will wrangle for religion, write for it; fight for it; die for it; anything but live for it.

Charles Colton

I've come to view Jesus much the way I view Elvis. I love the guy, but the fan clubs really freak me out.

John Fugelsang

BUSINESS & MONEY

Never economize on luxuries.

Angela Thirkell

People who say money can't buy you happiness just don't know where to shop.

Tara Palmer Tomkinson

Imagine six apartments. It isn't so hard to do; one is full of fur coats, the others full of shoes

Elton John, 40th birthday card message to John Lennon

There are few sorrows, however poignant, in which a good income is of no avail.

L.P. Smith

Always suspect any job men willingly vacate for women.

Jill Tweedie

Sexual harassment at work. Is it a problem for the self-employed?

Victoria Wood

Lack of money is the root of all evil.

George Bernard Shaw

Saving is a very fine thing, especially when your parents have done it for you.

Winston Churchill

I yield to no one in my admiration for the office as a social center, but it's no place actually to get any work done.

Katherine Whitehorn

He was so mean, he only breathed in.

Bob Monkhouse

The salesman who sold me the car told me I'd get a lot of pleasure out of it. He was right. It was a pleasure to get out of it.

Les Dawson

Bankruptcy is like losing your virginity. It doesn't hurt the next time.

Clarissa Dickson-Wright

One of the symptoms of an approaching nervous breakdown is the belief that one's work is terribly important.

Bertrand Russell

They say a woman's work is never done. Maybe that's why they get paid less.

Sean Lock

Happy is the man with a wife to tell him what to do and a secretary to do it.

Lord Stormont Mancroft

The man with a toothache thinks everyone happy whose teeth are sound. The poverty-stricken man makes the same mistake about the rich man.

George Bernard Shaw

❦

The value of money is that with it we can tell any man to go to the devil. It is the sixth sense which enables you to enjoy the other five.

W. Somerset Maugham

❦

The amount of money some parents want to spend . . . would enable baby Jesus to leave the stable and check in to a five-star hotel.

Ed Watson, on nativity play costumes

❦

I've just heard the best definition of English meanness. A friend has a weekend cottage in the country, with a bit of a garden. He hangs up bird feeders because he likes the sound and the flutter. Before he leaves on Sunday, he takes them down and puts them in the shed.

A.A. Gill

❦

Multitasking is the ability to screw everything up simultaneously.

Jeremy Clarkson

- What is two and two?

- Are you buying or selling?

Small child and Lew Grade

The one phrase it is imperative to know in every foreign language is: my friend will pay.

Alan Whicker

Had an amazing cab driver. He was smiling and whistling – clearly in a brilliant mood. He said, "I love my job, I'm my own boss. Nobody tells me what to do." I said, "Left here."

Jimmy Carr

Half the money my company has spent on advertising was wasted. The problem is to find out which half.

Lord Leverhulme

I just realized that 'Let me check my calendar' is the adult version of 'Let me ask my mom.'

Noelle Chatham

Robin Hood is my hero. Have I robbed the rich and given the poor? Well, half of that.

Lee Hurst

Actually, I have no regard for money. Aside from its purchasing power, it's completely useless as far as I'm concerned.

Alfred Hitchcock

Victoria pointed to her necklace and said, "£1.5 million." David introduced himself. I was staring at his wife's tits and shouting. "How much?"

Graham Norton, on meeting David and Victoria Beckham

Economics is the systematic complication of the simple truths of housekeeping.

Philip Howard

The end... almost!

Reviews are not easy to come by. As an independent author with a tiny marketing budget, I rely on readers, like you, to leave a short review on Amazon. Even if it's just a sentence or two!

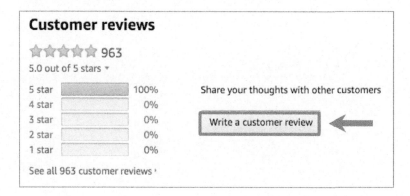

So if you enjoyed the book, please...

>> Click here to leave a brief review on Amazon.

I am very appreciative for your review as it truly makes a difference. Many thanks for purchasing this book and reading it to the end!

MISCELLANEOUS

The best piece of advice I ever received was: "Don't do it again."

Lord Cudlipp

The only statistics you can trust are those you falsified yourself.

Winston Churchill

I have one golden rule: I ask myself what Nanny would have expected me to do.

Lord Carrington

Don't give a woman advice: one should never give a woman anything she can't wear in the evening.

Oscar Wilde

Experts have spent years developing weapons which can destroy people's lives but leave the buildings intact. They're called mortgages.

Jeremy Hardy

Housekeeping is like being caught in a revolving door.

Marcelene Cox

I was once paged at JFK airport as "Mr. No One."

Peter Noone

Never spit in a man's face unless his mustache is on fire.

Henry Root

I always tell a young man not to use the word "always".

Robert Walpole

History will be kind to me, for I intend to write it.

Winston Churchill

Maybe this world is another planet's hell.

Aldous Huxley

It is not so much that the world that's got so much worse, but news coverage that's go so much better.

G.K. Chesterton

For there was never yet philosopher

That could bear the toothache patiently.

William Shakespeare

I have tried in my time to be a philosopher, but cheerfulness always kept breaking in.

Oliver Edwards

All philosophies, if you ride them home, are nonsense; but some are greater nonsense than others.

Samuel Butler

If God had intended men to smoke, he'd have put chimneys in their heads.

J. B. Priestley

⁌⁍

A good cigar is as great a comfort to a man as a good cry is to a woman.

Sir Edward Bulwer Lytton

⁌⁍

- Name a major disease associated with smoking.

- Premature death.

GCSE exam answer

⁌⁍

There are various ways to give up smoking – nicotine patches, nicotine gum. My auntie used to pour a gallon of petrol over herself every morning.

Paul Merton

⁌⁍

My mum told me I'd better get a toilet brush, so I did. I've been using it for a week, but I think I'm going back to paper.

Dave Spikey

⁌⁍

Give up smoking by sticking one cigarette from each new pack up a fat friend's arse, filter first, then replacing it in the box. The possibility of putting that one in your mouth will put off smoking any of them.

VIZ, Top tip

Madman are always serious; they go mad from lack of humor.

G.K. Chesterton

I didn't have a nervous breakdown. I was clinically fed up for two years.

Alan Partridge

The trouble with tranquilizers is that you find yourself being nice to the people you don't like.

Mark Bushman

The English climate: on a fine day, like looking up a chimney; on a rainy day, like looking down it.

Thomas Moore

Everybody talks about the weather, but nobody does anything about it.

Charles D. Warner

Ⓢ

I have no relish for the country; it is a kind of a healthy grave.

Sydney Smith

Ⓢ

Never join a queue unless you know what's at the end of it.

Gerald Challis

Ⓢ

The trouble with retirement is that you never get a day off.

Abe Lemons

Ⓢ

If you are going through hell, keep going.

Winston Churchill

Ⓢ

Know thyself – but don't tell anyone.

H. F. Henrichs

Ⓢ

500 Funny Quotes for Men

Inspirational Quotes to Boost Your Mood Instantly & Make Your Day A Little Happier!

Edited by Stan Hardy

PREFACE

Humor sticks the most with people, especially when it is short and contains some truth or life lessons. That is why funny quotes are so great! They allow us to take a quick break, relax, and take life a bit easier. We can also draw inspiration from them, knowing that Albert Einstein, Ernest Hemingway, Charlie Chaplin, or some other great minds had the same experiences and struggles as ours.

This uplifting book provides 500 funny quotes with some of the universal truisms that are part of our everyday lives. The spectrum of quotes is as diverse as they are funny. Whether it is a quote about Relationships, Children, Age, Sports, Fun, People, or Religion, reading these can't help but make one smile, think, learn from their wisdom, chuckle, and refresh.

You can enjoy this book by reading it cover to cover or by going directly to your topic of interest. The quotes are carefully selected from various sources and thousands of quotes. All efforts have been made to check the quotes' source and to use the correct attributions. If you are looking for some quality, inspirational, and funny quotes to brighten your day, this is the book for you! If this book made you smile, please take the time to leave a review to help future readers like yourself and help me as a publisher. You might as well enjoy my other work with 500 funny quotes for women.

Thank you for your time. I hope you will have lots of fun!

Stan Hardy

HOBBIES & FUN

A fishing rod is a stick with a hook at one side and a fool at the other.

Samuel Johnson

If you eliminate smoking and gambling, you will be amazed to find that almost all an Englishman's pleasures can be, and mostly are, shared by his dog.

George Bernard Shaw

Maybe the fish goes home and brags about the size of the bait he stole.

Gray Swan

Part of [the $10 million] went for gambling, horses, and women. The rest I spent foolishly.

George Raft, movie star

I can sympathize with people's pains, but not with their pleasure. There is something curiously boring about somebody else's happiness.

Aldous Huxley

This is really a lovely horse. I once rode her mother.

Ted Walsh, horseracing commentator

Women are really jealous of cigars . . . they regard them as a strong rival.

William Thackeray

Oscar Wilde has a legacy as being very witty. I don't think he was. I just think he talked all the time, and if you throw enough shit at the wall, some sticks.

Dan Atkinson

The fascination of shooting as a sport depends almost wholly on whether you are at the right or wrong end of the gun.

P.G. Wodehouse

Why is the sky blue? Because if it was green, an Englishman wouldn't know where to stop mowing.

Jack Harper

No man is a hypocrite in his pleasures.

Samuel Johnson

Most people would rather be certain they're miserable than risk being happy.

Robert Anthony

Do I examine myself for testicular cancer? I do. But I do it on the train.

Arthur Smith

The only exercise I take is walking behind the coffin of friends who took exercise.

Peter O'Toole

SPORT

Me and about eight mates went up Chelsea last February. Bill Clinton was bloody furious.

Frank Skinner

Golf is an ineffectual attempt to direct an uncontrollable sphere into an inaccessible hole with instruments ill-adapted to the purpose.

Winston Churchill

I never did like working out – it bears the same relationship to real sport as masturbation does to real sex.

David Lodge

The English football team – brilliant on paper, shit on grass.

Arthur Smith

If Stalin had learned to play cricket, the world might now be a better place.

Bishop Richard Downey

It is impossible to win gracefully at chess. No man has yet said "Mate!" in a voice which failed to sound to his opponent bitter, boastful and malicious.

A.A. Milne

A survey shows that English men are more afraid of watching England crash out of Euro 2004 on penalties than of losing their wallet, job, or even hair. Only losing a partner would cause greater distress than another penalty shootout disaster.

NEC Research

The ball is man's most disastrous invention, not excluding the wheel.

Robert Morley

Pitches are like wives; you never know how they're going to turn out.

Sir Len Hutton

Rugby is a good occasion for keeping 30 bullies far from the center of the city.

Oscar Wilde

You have to get your priorities right. Women are around all the time, but the World Cup comes only every four years.

Peter Osgood

Soccer is a simple-minded game for simple people; golf is merely an expensive way of leaving home.

Michael Parkinson

Golf balls are attracted to water as unerringly as the eye of a middle-aged man to a female bosom.

Michael Green

World Dart Players are beer-swilling, gold-chain-wearing, aftershave-reeking, 16-month-pregnant gentlemen (most of whom probably haven't seen their penises since last millennium) supported by the sort of women who only wear knickers to keep their feet warm.

Victor Lewis-Smith

Skiing is buying two thousand pounds of silly clothes and equipment and traveling a thousand miles through snow in a coach to stand around in a disco getting drunk.

Philip Howard

I don't play cricket. It requires one to adopt such indecent postures.

Oscar Wilde

Rowing seems to me to be a monotonous pursuit and somehow wasteful to be making all that effort to be going in the wrong direction.

Peter Ustinov

Driving a racing car is like lying in the bath with your feet on the taps but not as comfortable.

David Coulthard

SEX

Why do girls fake orgasms? Because they think we care.

Bob Geldof

Having therapy is very much like making love to a beautiful woman. You get on the couch, string 'em along with some half-lies and evasions, probe some deep dark holes, and then hand over all your money.

Swiss Toni (Charlie Higson), The Fast Show

An erection at will is the moral equivalent of a valid credit card.

Alex Comfort

Gentleman's wash: A hurried washing of the male genitals (usually in a pub toilet sink) in anticipation of forthcoming sex.

VIZ

There's only one good test of pornography. Get twelve normal men to read the book, and then ask them, "Did you get an erection?" If the answer is "Yes" from a majority of the twelve, then the book is pornographic.

W. H. Auden

A man's sperm count can be adversely affected by factors like heat, caffeine, and alcohol, so avoid dipping your plums in Irish coffee before sex.

Jeremy Hardy

I lost my virginity under a bridge. I was having sex with this poor girl, and I was trying my best, but I was like Scotland at a World Cup – just pleased to be there.

Russell Howard

Older women are best, because they always think they may be doing it for the last time.

Ian Fleming

A man with an erection is in no need of advice.

Samuel Pepys

The best women, like Rolls-Royces, should be delivered to the customer fully run in.

Leo Cooper

You girls would never help us boys out. You'd never undo the top button of your jeans. It was like trying to stroke a dog through a letterbox.

Jeff Green

The only reason my wife has an orgasm is so she'll have something else to moan about.

Bob Monkhouse

Lord Castlerosse was taken to task by Nancy Astor over the size of his stomach. "What would you say if that was on a woman?" she asked, pointedly. "Half an hour ago it was," he replied.

Nigel Rees

Sex

CHARACTER

An Englishman is a person who does things because they have been done before. An American is a person who does things because they haven't been done before.

Mark Twain

I am half British, half American. My passport has an eagle with a teabag in its beak.

Bob Hope

By his father he is English, by his mother he is American – to my mind the blend which makes the perfect man.

Mark Twain on Winston Churchill

If stupidity got us into this mess, then why can't it get us out?

Will Rogers

If you think you are too small to make a difference, try sleeping with a mosquito.

Dalai Lama

A person without a sense of humor is like a wagon without springs. It's jolted by every pebble on the road.

Henry Ward Beecher

My idea of an agreeable person is a person who agrees with me.

Benjamin Disraeli

I was going to sue for defamation of character, but then I realized I have no character.

Charles Barkley, TV basketball analyst

By all means let's be open-minded, but not so open-minded that our brains drop out.

Richard Dawkins, scientist

He was so narrow-minded, he could see through a keyhole with both eyes.

Molly Ivins, author

Two things are infinite: the universe and human stupidity, and I'm not sure about the universe.

Albert Einstein

In England, it is bad manners to be clever, to assert something confidently. It may be your personal view that two and two makes four, but you must not state it in a self-assured way because this is a democratic country, and others may be of a different opinion.

George Mikes

Remember the kettle, always up to its neck in hot water, yet it still sings.

English saying

All charming people have something to conceal, usually their total dependence on the appreciation of others.

Cyril Connolly

He can compress the most words into the smallest idea of any man I know.

Abraham Lincoln

He can compress the most words into the smallest idea of any man I know.

The important thing when you are going to do something brave is to have someone on hand to witness it.

Michael Howard

I dislike arguments of any kind. They are always vulgar and often convincing.

Oscar Wilde

They say a man should be judged by his enemies. I am very proud of mine.

Michael Heseltine, politician

He is a self-made man and worships his creator.

Henry Clapp, newspaper editor

The more things a man is ashamed of, the more respectable he is.

George Bernard Shaw

When I make a joke, I always laugh quickly, so that there's no doubt about it.

W. Somerset Maugham

I don't operate rationally. I think just like a woman.

James Dyson, inventor of Dyson vacuum cleaners

When a stupid man is doing something he is ashamed of, he always declares that it is his duty.

George Bernard Shaw

If the remarks with which I am credited - and never made – are really good, I acknowledge them. I generally work myself into the belief that I originally said them.

Noel Coward

It is only the dull that like practical jokes.

Oscar Wilde

❦

Blessed is he who expects nothing, for he shall not be disappointed.

Jonathan Swift

❦

An Englishman thinks he is moral when he is only uncomfortable.

George Bernard Shaw

❦

I am easily satisfied with the very best.

Winston Churchill

❦

A hero is one who is afraid to run away.

English proverb

❦

"I" is the most popular letter in the alphabet.

Oliver Herford

❦

When a man is wrapped up in himself, he makes a pretty small package.

John Ruskin

MEN, WOMEN & RELATIONSHIPS

I hate mankind, for I think myself as one of the best of them, and I know how bad I am.

Samuel Johnson

Before you criticize someone, you should walk a mile in their shoes. That way when you criticize them, you are a mile away from them and you have their shoes.

Jack Handey

Have you ever noticed that anybody driving faster than you is a maniac, and anyone going slower than you is a moron?

George Carlin

My advice to you is to get married: If you find a good wife, you'll be happy; if not, you'll become a philosopher.

Socrates

They say men can't multitask, but you watch us when we nearly get caught watching porn, we're like ninjas: telly over, trousers up, tissues down the couch.

Jason Manford

They say marriages are made in Heaven. But so is thunder and lightning.

Clint Eastwood.

I am a modern man. I've got no problem buying tampons. But apparently, women don't consider them a proper present.

Jimmy Carr

There are only three things to be done with a woman. You can love her, suffer for her or turn her into literature.

Lawrence Durrell

What would women do if they could not cry? What poor, defenseless creatures they would be.

Douglas Jerrold

Before you marry a person, you should first make them use a computer with slow Internet service to see who they really are.

Will Ferrell

There must be some reason why a man must be convinced, while a woman must be persuaded.

Robert Fleming

The trouble with women is that they never put the toilet seat back up.

Simon Nye

The main difference between men and women is that men are lunatics and women are idiots.

Rebecca West

Women are never disarmed by compliments. Men always are. That is the difference between the two sexes.

Oscar Wilde

The happiest marriage I can picture or imagine to myself would be the union of a deaf man to a blind woman.

Samuel Taylor Coleridge

Bigamy is having one wife too many. Monogamy is the same.

Oscar Wilde

If we men had periods, we wouldn't have discreet tampon boxes, would we? We'd have boxes with MY FUCKING TAMPONS printed on the outside.

Ben Elton

Love is blind, and marriage is the institution for the blind.

James Graham

A man's face is his autobiography. A woman's face is her work of fiction.

Oscar Wilde

The greatest mistake is trying to be more agreeable than you can be.

Walter Bagehot

It has been said that man is a rational animal. All my life I have been searching for evidence which could support this.

Bertrand Russell

I would never be unfaithful to my wife for the simple reason that I love my house too much.

Bob Monkhouse

Bachelors should be heavily taxed. It is not fair that some men should be happier than others.

Oscar Wilde

Swans mate for life, and look how bad-tempered they are.

Jeff Green

Never exaggerate your faults. Your friends will attend to that.

Francis Bacon, philosopher

❦

American women expect to find in their husbands a perfection that English women only hope to find in their butlers.

W. Somerset Maugham

❦

I've had bad luck with both my wives. The first one left me, and the second one didn't.

Patrick Murray

❦

Men marry because they are tired; women because they are curious. Both are disappointed.

Oscar Wilde

❦

Strategy is buying a bottle of fine wine when you take a lady out for dinner. Tactics is getting her to drink it.

Frank Muir

❦

A true friend is one who likes you despite your achievements.

Arnold Bennett

⁂

The important thing when you are going to do something brave is to have someone on hand to witness it.

Michael Howard

⁂

You have to come up with this shit every year. Last week I just wrote, "I still love you, see last year's card for full details."

Michael McIntyre, on Valentine's Day cards

⁂

Don't marry for money; you can borrow it cheaper.

Scottish proverb

⁂

A woman is never shy of patting you on the tummy and saying, "Who ate all the pies, Peter?" You're supposed to say, "Ha, ha! Yes I'm a fat old git, aren't I?" But do the same to a woman and die.

Peter Davison

⁂

It is absurd to divide people into good and bad. People are either charming or tedious.

Oscar Wilde

The English are polite by telling lies. The Americans are polite by telling the truth.

Malcolm Bradbury

Women think we are normal ... But all the time in our brains we've got the word "breasts" on a loop. If we ever lost control for a second, we'd all start shouting, "breasts, breasts, breasts, breaastsss ..."

Jeff Murdock (Richard Coyle), Coupling

He has no enemies, but is intensely disliked by his friends.

Oscar Wilde

It is assumed that a woman must wait motionless until she is wooed. That is how the spider waits for the fly.

George Bernard Shaw

The closest to perfection a person ever comes is when he fills out a job application.

Stanley Randall

Biologically speaking, if something bites you, it is more likely to be female.

Desmond Morris

A cynic is a man who knows the prices of everything and the value of nothing.

Oscar Wilde

A person who is keen to shake your hand, usually has something up his sleeve.

Alec Guinness

I sometimes think that God, in creating man, overestimated his ability.

Oscar Wilde

The only consolation I can find in your immediate presence is your ultimate absence.

Shelagh Delaney

Aristotle maintained that women have fewer teeth than men; although he was twice married, it never occurred to him to verify this statement by examining his wives' mouth.

Bertrand Russel

An economist is someone who, if you have forgotten your telephone number, will estimate it for you.

Frank Morton

Women never look so well as when one comes in wet and dirty from hunting.

R.S. Surtees

I haven't spoken to my wife for over a month. We haven't had a row – it's just that I'm afraid to interrupt her.

Les Dawson

I hate nobody except Hitler – and that is professional.

Winston Churchill

The Bible tells us to love our neighbors, and also to love our enemies; probably because they are generally the same people.

G. K. Chesterton

My girlfriend says, "You never tell me how much you love me." I don't want to upset her.

Jimmy Carr

- If you were my wife, I'd put poison in your coffee.

- If I were your husband, I'd drink it.

Nancy Astor and Winston Churchill

- Which do you think is my best side?

- My dear, you're sitting on it.

Mary Anderson (actress) and Alfred Hitchcock

Brigands demand your money or your life; women require both.

Samuel Butler

Having a wedding without mentioning divorce is like sending someone to war without mentioning that people are going to get killed.

Richard Curtis

- Mr. Churchill, I care neither for your politics nor your mustache.

- Do not distress yourself, madam, you are unlikely to come into contact with either.

Unidentified woman and Winston Churchill

Men play the game; women know the score.

Roger Woddis

I have often wanted to drown my troubles, but I can't get my wife to go swimming.

Roy "Chubby" Brown

My best mate's girlfriend is six months pregnant. She said to me, "Do you want to feel the baby?" On reflection, I think she meant on the outside.

Jimmy Carr

A man can be happy with any woman as long as he does not love her.

Oscar Wilde

- Winston, you are drunk, and what's more, you are disgustingly drunk.

- Bessie, my dear, you are ugly, and what's more, you are disgustingly ugly. But tomorrow I shall be sober and you will still be disgustingly ugly.

Bessie Braddock and Winston Churchill

I couldn't believe it the other day when I picked up a British newspaper and read that 82 percent of men would rather sleep with a goat than me.

Sara Ferguson, The Duchess of York

Sphinxes without secrets.

Oscar Wilde on women

Perhaps hate is recycled love.

Jeffrey Bernard

The penalty for getting the woman is that you must keep her.

Lionel Strachey

What attracts us in a woman rarely binds us to her.

John Collins

Parents are the last people on earth who ought to have children.

Samuel Butler

The extreme penalty for bigamy? Two mothers-in-law.

Lord Chief Justice Russell

After I won the Million Dollar Challenge in South Africa, I asked my wife if she'd like a Versace dress, diamonds or pearls as a present, but she said, "No!" When I asked her what she did want, she said, "A divorce," but I told her I wasn't intending to spend that much.

Nick Faldo

ART & CULTURE

- Mr. Churchill, I want you to know I got up at dawn and drove a hundred miles for the unveiling of your bust.

- Madam, I want you to know that I would happily reciprocate the honor.

Unidentified woman and Winston Churchill

I am amazed at radio DJs today. I am firmly convinced that AM on my radio stands for Absolute Moron. I will not begin to tell you what FM stands for.

Jasper Carrott

If it were not for the intellectual snobs who pay – in solid cash – the arts would perish with their starving practitioners. Let us thank Heaven for hypocrisy.

Aldous Huxley

My main reason for adopting literature as a profession was that, as the author is never seen by his clients, he need not dress respectably.

George Bernard Shaw

❧

Television? No good will come of this device. The word is half Greek and half Latin.

C.P. Scott

❧

News is what someone wants to suppress; anything else is just advertising.

Lord Northcliffe

❧

As I was leaving this morning, I said to myself, "The last thing you must do is forget your speech." And, sure enough, as I left the house this morning, the last thing I did was to forget my speech.

Rowan Atkinson

❧

No news is good news; no journalism is even better news.

Nicholas Bentley

❧

There's never any graffiti in the hotel. Although in the Gents a couple of weeks ago, I did see someone had drawn a lady's part. Quite detailed. The guy obviously had talent.

Alan Partridge (a.k.a. Steve Coogan)

The English public take no interest in a work of art until it is told that the work in question is immoral.

Oscar Wilde

A good film is when the price of the dinner, the theatre admission, and the babysitter were worth it.

Alfred Hitchcock

There is nothing so terrible as the pursuit of arts by those who have no talent.

W. Somerset Maugham

The good ended happily, and the bad unhappily. That is what Fiction means.

Oscar Wilde

What literature can and should do is change the people who teach the people who don't read the books.

A.S. Byatt

All rock & roll singers sound like a nudist backing into a cold-nosed dog – set to music.

Robert Orben

I cannot choose one hundred best books because I have written only five.

Oscar Wilde

Hell is full of musical amateurs.

George Bernard Shaw

All fiction is largely autobiographical and much autobiography is, of course, fiction.

P.D. James

Other people's troubles are mostly what folks read the paper for, and it's twice the pleasure when it's the trouble of a man they know.

Harold Brighouse

The really interesting thing about James Bond is that he would be what I call the ideal defector. Because if the money was better, the booze freer, and the women easier over there in Moscow, he'd be off like a shot. Bond, you see, is the ultimate prostitute.

John Le Carre

In America, journalism is apt to be regarded as an extension of history; in Britain, as an extension of conversation.

Anthony Sampson

I prefer painting landscapes. A tree doesn't complain that I haven't done it justice.

Winston Churchill

Explaining how you write poetry ... it's like going around explaining how you sleep with your wife.

Philip Larkin

What readers ask nowadays in a book is that it should improve, instruct, and elevate. My book wouldn't elevate a cow.

Jerome K. Jerome

A poet can survive everything but a misprint.

Oscar Wilde

Books are like mirrors: if a fool looks in, you cannot expect a genius to look out.

J.K. Rowling

My roles play into a certain fantasy of what people want English people to be, whereas half the time we're vomiting beer and beating people up.

Hugh Grant

A newspaper consists of the same number of words whether there be any news in it or not.

Henry Fielding

I love Wagner's music much better than anybody's. It is so loud that one can talk the whole time without other people hearing what one says. That is a great advantage.

Oscar Wilde

Shakespeare's stuff is different from mine, but that is not to say that it is inferior.

P.G. Wodehouse

Television is the first truly democratic culture – the first culture available to everybody and entirely governed by what the people want. The most terrifying thing is what people do want.

Clive Barnes

I can take any amount of criticism, so long as it is unqualified praise.

Noel Coward

Your manuscript is both good and original; but the part that is good is not original, and the part that is original is not good.

Samuel Johnson

We're more popular than Jesus Christ now. I don't know which will go first. Rock & roll or Christianity.

John Lennon

I always knew that if all else failed I could become an actor – and all else failed.

David Niven

Voltaire said that what was too silly to be said could be sung. Now you seem to think that what is too delicate to be said can be whistled.

George Bernard Shaw

The remarkable thing about television is that it permits several million people to laugh at the same joke and still feel lonely.

T.S. Eliot

When I played drunk, I had to remain sober because I didn't know how to play them when I was drunk.

Richard Burton

The more I read Socrates, the less I wonder that they poisoned him.

Thomas Babington Macaulay

A critic is a man who knows the way but can't drive the car.

Kenneth Tynan

Journalism is the ability to meet the challenge of filling space.

Rebecca West

- How do you rate your music?

- We're not good musicians. Just adequate.

- Then why are you so popular.

- Maybe people like adequate music.

Interviewer and The Beatles

Art & Culture

MANNERS

An Englishman, even if he is alone, forms an orderly queue of one.

George Mikes

No one can be as calculatedly rude as the British, which amazes Americans, who do not understand studied insult.

Paul Gallico

Thank you for the manuscript; I shall lose no time in reading it.

Benjamin Disraeli

A good way to start a speech is to say: "As Henry VIII said to his wives: "I won't keep you long.""

Sir Claus Moser

Let your enemies be disarmed by the gentleness of your manner, but at the same time let them feel the steadiness of your resentment.

Lord Chesterfield

In France, it is rude to let a conversation drop; in England, it is rash to keep it up. No one there will blame you for silence. When you have not opened your mouth for three years, they will think: "This Frenchman is a nice quiet fellow."

Andre Maurios

In England, the art of conversation consists of knowing when to keep silent.

Pierre Daninos

The Englishman, be it noted, seldom resorts to violence; when he is sufficiently goaded, he simply opens up, like the oyster, and devours his adversary.

Henry Miller

She fell down a lift shaft on Ascension Day – so perverse of her.

Noel Coward

All Englishman talk as if they've got a bushel of plums stuck in their throats, and then after swallowing them get constipated with the pits.

W.C. Fields

The great secret is not having bad manners or good manners or having any other particular sort of manners, but having the same manner for all the human soul; in short, behaving as if you were in Heaven, where there are no third-class carriages and one soul is as good as another.

George Bernard Shaw

If I am a gentleman and you are a gentleman, who will milk the cow?

Irish proverb

The fact that I am not a millionaire aristocrat with the sexual capacity of a rutting rhino is a constant niggle.

Edmund Blackadder, Blackadder III

I never queue. I wouldn't queue for a seat at the Last Supper, with the original cast.

Robert Helpman

People who think they know everything are a great annoyance to those of us who do.

Isaac Asimov, science fiction writer

LANGUAGE

It is impossible for an Englishman to open his mouth without making another Englishman hate him or despise him.

George Bernard Shaw

I will not instruct my daughters in foreign languages. One tongue is sufficient for a woman.

John Milton

As far as I'm concerned, 'whom' is a word that was invented to make everyone sound like a butler.

Calving Trillin

The word papa gives a pretty form to the lips. Papa, potatoes, poultry, prunes, and prism are all good words for the lips.

Charles Dickens

I was criticized for swearing on television. The word I used was "bloody", which, where I come from in Yorkshire, is practically the only surviving adjective.

Maureen Lipman

Euphemisms are unpleasant truths wearing diplomatic cologne.

Quentin Crisp

If you want a linguistic adventure, go drinkin' with a Scotsman. Casue if you thought you couldn't understand him before…

Robin Williams

I am the most spontaneous speaker in the world because every word, every gesture, and every retort has been carefully rehearsed.

George Bernard Shaw

Translations (like wives) are seldom faithful if they are in the least attractive.

Roy Campbell

American is the language in which people say what they mean, as Italian is the language in which they say what they feel. English is the language in which what a character means or feels has to be deduced from what he or she says, which may be quite the opposite.

John Mortimer

When BBC first broadcast to the USA, it took a team of translators a week to figure out that "bangers and mash" were not some veiled British threat.

Bill Clinton

- Was death instant?

- Instantaneous, Lewis. Coffee may be instant, death may not.

Sergeant Lewis & Inspector Morse, Inspector Morse

BURMA: Be Upstairs Ready My Angel

NORWICH: Knickers Off Ready When I Come Home

POLO: Pants Off, Legs Open

Acronyms

Everybody has the right to pronounce foreign names as he chooses.

Winston Churchill

LUCK & HAPPINESS

God not only plays dice. He also sometimes throws them where they cannot be seen.

Stephen Hawking

To be without some of the things you want is a vital part of happiness.

Bertrand Russell

Some folk want their luck buttered.

Thomas Hardy

If any of you cry at my funeral, I'll never speak to you again.

Stan Laurel

I'm not happy. But I'm not unhappy about it.

Alan Bennett

❧

Sometimes you lie in bed at night, and you don't have a single thing to worry about. That always worries me!

Charlie Brown

❧

Instant gratification takes too long.

Carrie Fisher

❧

This lamentable phrase, "the pursuit of happiness," is responsible for a good part of the ills and miseries of the modern world.

Malcolm Muggeridge

❧

Men who are unhappy, like the men who sleep badly, are always proud of the fact.

Bertrand Russell

❧

Time misspent in youth is sometimes all the freedom one ever has.

Anita Brookner

The formula for complete happiness is to be very busy with the unimportant.

A. Edward Newton

If there were in the world today any large number of people who desired their own happiness more than they desired the unhappiness of others, we could have paradise in a few years.

Bertrand Russell

Always laugh when you can. It is cheap medicine.

Lord Byron

A short message from the Editor

Hey, hope you're enjoying the book. I'd love to hear your thoughts!

Many readers do not know how hard reviews are to come by, and how much they help an author.

I would be incredibly thankful if you could take just 60 seconds to write a brief review on Amazon, even if it's just a few sentences!

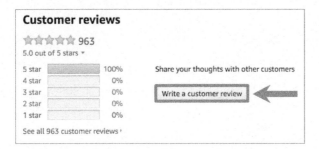

Please scan the QR code below to leave your review:

Thank you for taking the time to share your thoughts!

Your review will genuinely make a difference for me and help gain exposure for my work.

Food & Diet

It's easy to distract fat people. A piece of cake.

Chris Addison

The Japanese eat very little fat and suffer fewer heart attacks than the British or Americans. The French eat a lot of fat and also have fewer heart attacks than the British or Americans. The Japanese drink very little red wine and suffer fewer heart attacks than the British or Americans. The Italians drink excessive amounts of red wine and also suffer fewer heart attacks than the British or Americans. Conclusion: eat or drink what you like. What kills you is speaking English.

Michael Fitzpatrick

Everything I eat has been proved by some doctor or other to be a deadly poison, and everything I don't eat has been proved to be indispensable for life.

George Bernard Shaw

Floating in his pool, he was just the reverse of an iceberg – 90 percent of him was visible.

Peter Ustinov

American-style iced tea is the perfect drink for a hot, sunny day. It's never really caught on in the UK, probably because the last time we had a hot, sunny day was back in 1957.

Tom Holt

"This coffee tastes like mud," I said. "I'm not surprised," the waitress said, "it was only ground this morning."

Les Dawson

Great restaurants are, of course, nothing but mouth-brothels. There is no point in going to them if one intends to keep one's belt buckled.

Frederic Raphael

A lot of people cry when they chop onions. The trick is not to form an emotional bond.

Jimmy Carr

The lighting in a restaurant should be dark enough to be discreet, light enough for a short-sighted person to read a menu, and not quite so light as to let people read the prices without looking most carefully.

Clement Freud

A mind of the caliber of mine cannot derive its nutriment from cows.

George Bernard Shaw

Hardcore vegetarians won't drive through towns with "ham" in the name.

Bill Bailey

As accurately as I can calculate, between the age of 10 and 70, I have eaten 44 wagon-load of food more than was good for me.

Sydney Smith

He who does not mind his belly, will hardly mind anything else.

Samuel Johnson

We may find in the long run that tinned food is a deadlier weapon than the machine-gun.

George Orwell, 1937

I knew a cannibal who had been influenced by Catholic missionaries. On Fridays, he ate only fisherman.

Tommy Cooper

In England, an elevator is called a "lift", a mile is called a "kilometer", and botulism is called "steak and kidney pie".

Marge Simpson, THE SIMPSONS

There is no love sincerer than the love of food.

George Bernard Shaw

Lord Northcliffe: Looking at how thin you are, people would think there was a famine in England.

George Bernard Shaw: And looking at how fat you are, people would think you were the cause of it.

FASHION & BEAUTY

Mr. Jones, the landlord of the 300-year-old Rose and Crown, said: "One Belgian tried to strangle me. I didn't mind him at my throat, but I took exception to a drunken foreigner grabbing my 1st Airborne Division tie."

Daily Mirror

With an evening coat and a white tie, anybody, even a stockbroker, can gain a reputation for being civilized.

Oscar Wilde

Bow-ties: are you a gay professor? Then take it off.

David Quantick

Yes, I wear spectacles, but only for reading and seeing things.

Ronnie Barker

I'm not saying my wife's ugly but she went to see that film, The Elephant Man, and the audience thought he was making a personal appearance.

Les Dawson

Single bagger: a lady so ugly she needs a bag on the head.

Double bagger: a lady so ugly that she needs a bag on her head and so do you in case hers falls off.

British Army slang

Did you see her boob job? You don't wanna drive around in an old Transit just because it's got new headlamps.

Ripley Holden, Blackpool

He had but one eye, and the popular prejudice runs in favor of two.

Charles Dickens

It is only shallow people who do not judge by appearances.

Oscar Wilde

I knew I was going bald when it was taking longer and longer to wash my face.

Harry Hill

Fashion & Beauty

DRUGS & ALCOHOL

I've never had a problem with drugs. I've had problems with the police.

Keith Richards

Martinis before lunch are like a woman's breasts. One is too few and three are too many.

John Humphrys

Soon after my grandmother's death, we were amused to find among odds and ends in her dressing-table drawer a bottle labeled "Might be Aspirin."

Jean Gibbs

What's my view on drugs? I've forgotten my view on drugs.

Boris Johnson, MP, campaigning in the 2005 election

Come on, Manny. You can find work and sort your life out anytime. The pub closes in five hours.

Bernard Black, Black Books

I'm on so many pills, I'll need a childproof lid on my coffin.

Paul O'Grady

The most important thing to remember about drunks is that drunks are far more intelligent than non-drunks. They spend a lot of time talking in pubs, unlike workaholics, who concentrate on their careers and ambitions, who never develop their higher spiritual values, who never explore the insides of their head like a drunk does.

Shane MacGowan

I only take a drink on two occasions – when I'm thirsty and when I'm not.

Brendan Behan

Compromises are for relationships, not wine.

Sir Robert Scott Caywood

I'm on a whisky diet. I've lost three days already.

Tommy Cooper

Man, the creature who knows he must die, who has dreams larger than his destiny, who is forever working a confidence trick on himself, needs an ally. Mine has been tobacco.

J.B. Priestley

One of the disadvantages of wine is that it makes a man mistake words for thoughts.

Samuel Johnson

Drunkenness is temporary suicide.

Bertrand Russell

Trying to separate cigarettes and alcohol, that's against God's will!

Ed Byrne

We don't know much about the human conscience, except that it is soluble in alcohol.

John Mortimer

Alcohol is a very necessary article . . . It makes life bearable to millions of people who could not endure their existence if they were quite sober. It enables Parliament to do things at eleven at night that no sane person would do at eleven in the morning.

George Bernard Shaw

All I can say is that I have taken more out of alcohol than alcohol has taken out of me.

Winston Churchill

Malt does more than Milton can,

To justify God's ways to man.

A. E. Housman

Too young to die. Too drunk to live.

Renee McCall on Brendan Behan

I haven't touched a drop of alcohol since the invention of the funnel.

Malachy McCourt

Sir, - The Publishers, Michael Joseph, have asked me to write my autobiography and I'd be grateful if you could give me any information about my whereabouts and behavior between 1960 and 1974.

Jeffrey Bernard, Letter in the New Stateman, 1975

Dear Mr. Bernard, - I read with interest your letter asking for information as to your whereabouts and behavior between 1960-74. On a certain evening in September 1969, you rang my mother to inform her that you were going to murder her only son. If you would like further information, I can put you in touch with many people who have enjoyed similar bizarre experiences in your company. Yours sincerely.

Michael J. Molloy, Editor of the Daily Mirror, 1975

I once asked an alcoholic doctor how did he first know he was an alcoholic, and he told me, "When I sprayed vaginal deodorant on a man's face".

Jeffrey Bernard

I couldn't go to the AA meetings. I couldn't drive. I was too drunk.

Frank Skinner

I am a strict teetotaler. I never take anything between drinks.

James Joyce

I formed a new group called Alcoholics-Unanimous. If you don't feel like a drink, you ring another member and he comes over to persuade you.

Richard Harris

I don't know why you need to smell wine before you drink it; you don't listen to a CD and rub it to your ear beforehand.

Michael McIntyre

POLITICS

Power is like a woman you want to stay in bed with forever.

Patrick Anderson

No lover ever studied every whim of his mistress as I did those of President Roosevelt

Winston Churchill

Politics is the art of making the inevitable seem planned.

Quentin Crisp

The trouble with political jokes is they get elected.

Tim Brooke-Taylor

The Democrats are the party that says Government will make you smarter, taller, richer, and remove the crabgrass on your lawn.

P. J. O'Rourke, writer

The Republicans are the party that says Government doesn't work, and then they get elected and prove it.

P. J. O'Rourke, still a writer

To those of you who received honors, awards and distinctions, I say well done. And to the C students, I say you, too, can be president of the United States.

George W. Bush

When you have bacon in your mouth, it doesn't matter who's president.

Louis CK

"The truth" in politics means any statement that cannot be proved false.

Sir Humphrey Appleby, Yes, Prime Minister

Distrust of authority should be the first civic duty.

Norman Douglas

We ought to have declared war on Germany the moment Mr. Hitler's police stole Einstein's violin.

George Bernard Shaw

The difference between a misfortune and a calamity is this: if Gladstone fell into the Thames, it would be a misfortune. But if someone dragged him out again, that would be a calamity.

Benjamin Disraeli

Never believe anything until it has been officially denied.

Claud Cockburn

It's no good telling the politicians to go to hell because they're building it for us.

Les Dawson

Socialism is the Government of the duds, by the duds, and for the duds.

Winston Churchill

Democracy consists of choosing your dictators after they've told you what you think it is you want to hear.

Alan Coren

In 1933, Hitler held his first Nuremberg rally (not a driving event), not to be confused with the later Nuremberg Trials (not a riding event).

Jo Brand

Men enter local politics solely as a result of being unhappily married.

C. Northcote Parkinson

I'm all in favor of free expression, provided it's kept rigidly under control.

Alan Bennett

You cannot make a man by standing a sheep on its hind legs. But by standing a flock of sheep in that position you can make a crowd of men.

Max Beerbohm

He knows nothing and he thinks he knows everything. That points clearly to a political career.

George Bernard Shaw

We have a system of Government with the engine of a lawnmower and the brakes of a Rolls-Royce.

Jonathan Lynn

Democracy is a device that ensures we shall be governed no better than we deserve.

George Bernard Shaw

We should silence anyone who opposes the right to freedom of speech.

Boyle Roche

There's as much chance of my becoming Prime Minister as there is of finding Elvis on Mars, or my being decapitated by a frisbee or reincarnated as an olive.

Boris Johnson

Civil servants – no longer servants, no longer civil.

Winston Churchill

❦

Democracy means government by discussion, but it is only effective if you can stop people talking.

Clement Attlee

❦

It's not the voting that's democracy, it's the counting.

Tom Stoppard

❦

If there were 20 ways of telling the truth and only one way of telling a lie, the Government would find it. It's in the nature of governments to tell lies.

George Bernard Shaw

❦

If you are working class, being an MP is the job your parents always wanted for you. It's clean, indoor, and there is no heavy lifting.

Diane Abbott

❦

All political parties die at last, swallowing their own lies.

John Arbuthnot

- Vote for you? I'd rather vote for the Devil!

- But in case your friend is not running, may I count on your support?

A voter and Winston Churchill

I could never be a politician. I couldn't bear to be right all the time.

Peter Ustinov

If he can't ignore the facts, he's no business to be a politician.

Sir Humphrey Appleby, Yes, Prime Minister

I am humble enough to recognize that I have made mistakes but politically astute enough to know that I have forgotten what they are.

Michael Heseltine

Political ability is the ability to foretell what is going to happen tomorrow, next week, next month, and next year. And to have the ability afterwards to explain why it didn't happen.

Winston Churchill

We should always tell the Press, freely and frankly, anything that they can easily find out.

Sir Humphrey Appleby, Yes, Prime Minister

The inherent vice of capitalism is the unequal sharing of blessings; the inherent virtue of socialism is the equal sharing of miseries.

Winston Churchill

SCIENCE

Why does the universe go to all the bother of existing?

Stephen Hawking

I almost think it is the ultimate destiny of science to exterminate the human race.

Thomas Love Peacock

I think computer viruses should count as life. I think it says something about human nature that the only form of life we have created so far is purely destructive. We've created life in our own image.

Stephen Hawking

For every expert, there is an equal and opposite expert.

Arthur C. Clarke

I heard that Jesus had a pet dinosaur. Evolution must be a myth, then.

John Bacon

⸙

If evolution really works, how come mothers only have two hands?

Milton Berle

⸙

The great tragedy of science: the slaying of a beautiful hypothesis by an ugly fact.

Thomas Huxley

⸙

I always wanted to be an inventor, like my dad – he also wanted to be an inventor.

Katie Schutte

⸙

Personally, I rather look forward to a computer program winning the world chess championship. Humanity needs a lesson in humility.

Richard Dawkins

⸙

Every revolutionary idea seems to evoke three stages of reaction. They may be summed up by the phrases: (1) It's completely impossible. (2) It's possible, but it's not worth doing. (3) I said it was a good idea all along.

Arthur C. Clarke

I believe the souls of five hundred Sir Isaac Newton would go to the making up of a Shakespeare or a Milton

Samuel Taylor Coleridge

The idea that life was put together by a random shuffling of constituent molecules can be shown to be ridiculous and improbable as the proposition that a tornado blowing through a junk yard might assemble a Boeing 747 from the materials therein.

Sir Fred Hoyle

Science is simply common sense at its best.

Thomas Huxley

User: the word computer professionals use when they mean 'idiot.'

Dave Barry

Any sufficiently advanced technology is indistinguishable from magic.

Arthur C. Clarke

The moment fire was invented, men didn't say, "Hey, let's cook!" They said, "Great! Now we can see naked women in the dark."

Steve Taylor, Coupling

BUSINESS & MONEY

Three things in life are certain: death, taxes, and more meetings.

Simon Jenkins

Credit is a system whereby a person who cannot pay gets another person who cannot pay to guarantee that he can pay.

Charles Dickens

People say I wasted my money. I say 90 percent went on women, fast cars, and booze. The rest I wasted.

George Best

Always borrow money from a pessimist. He won't expect it back.

Oscar Wilde

One man's wage rise is another man's price increase.

Harold Wilson

Filling out a credit card application, my friend came upon this question: 'What is your source of income?' She wrote: 'ATM.'

Michael Mcrae

Reading computer manuals without the hardware is as frustrating as reading a sex manual without the software.

Arthur C. Clarke

No rich man considers himself rich enough, but I consider myself poor enough.

George Mikes

A citizen can hardly distinguish between a tax and a fine, except that the fine is generally much lighter.

G.K. Chesterton

A little inaccuracy sometimes saves tons of explanation.

Hector Hugh Munro

It's all in the marketing – if you call the economic slowdown a recession, it sounds bad. If you call it the credit crunch, it sounds like a new flavor of ice cream by Ben & Jerry's.

Ed Byrne

I am going to start at the bottom and work my way down.

P.G. Wodehouse

A man explained inflation to his wife thus: "When we married, you measured 36-24-36. Now you're 42-42-42. There's more of you, but you are not worth as much."

Lord Barnett

For a nation to try to tax itself into prosperity is like a man standing in a bucket and trying to lift himself up by the handle.

Winston Churchill

There are few things in this world more assuring than an unhappy lottery winner.

Tony Parsons

A judge said that all his experience both as Counsel and Judge has been spent sorting out the difficulties of people who, upon the recommendation of people they did not know, signed documents which they did not read, to buy goods they did not need, with money they had not got.

Gilbert Harding

I wouldn't say I was the best manager in the business, but I was in the Top One.

Brian Clough

CRIME & PUNISHMENT

In law, nothing is certain but the expense.

Samuel Butler

Nobody ever commits a crime without doing something stupid.

Oscar Wilde

Guns don't kill people, people kill people, and monkeys do too – if they have a gun.

Eddie Izzard

Can you imagine a world without men? No crime and lots of happy fat women.

Nicole Hollander, cartoonist.

Laws are like cobwebs, which may catch small flies, but let wasps and hornets breakthrough.

Jonathan Swift

There are only about 20 murders committed a year in London and not all are serious – some are just husbands killing their wives.

G.H. Hatherill

If you can keep your head when all about are losing theirs, you'll be taller than anybody else.

Tim Brooke-Taylor

CAR THIEVES OPERATE IN THIS AREA. Where else would they operate? It's a fucking car park! The number of times I've been driving through the country, see a couple of car thieves standing in a field saying "You said there'd be cars!"

Lee Evans

I've always thought the best thing to do if you hear a burglar is to get stark naked, working on the assumption that no burglar will think there's any possession worth nicking that you've got to wrestle a naked man for.

Jeff Green

LIFE & DEATH

Sometimes I wonder if we don't actually prefer things a little crap.

Ben Elton

My talent I put into my writing; my genius I have saved for living.

Oscar Wilde

Life is what happens to you while you're busy making other plans.

John Lennon

I would never die for my beliefs because I might be wrong.

Bertrand Russell

The reports of my death are greatly exaggerated.

Mark Twain

I know a man who gave up smoking, drinking, sex, and rich food. He was healthy right up to the day he killed himself.

Johnny Carson

Blame someone else and get on with your life.

Alan Woods

When I die, I want to die like my grandfather, who died peacefully in his sleep. Not screaming like all the passengers in his car.

Will Rogers

I have noticed that even people who claim everything is pre-determined and that we can do nothing to change it look before they cross the road.

Stephen Hawking, physicist

According to most studies, people's number one fear is public speaking. Number two is death. Death is number two. Does that seem right? That means to the average person, if you have to go to a funeral, you're better off in the casket than doing the eulogy.

Jerry Seinfeld

Life is a wretched grey Saturday, but it has to be lived through.

Anthony Burgess

When I look back on all these worries, I remember the story of the old man who said on his deathbed that he had had a lot of troubles in his life, most of which never happened.

Winston Churchill

My only regret in life is that I did not drink more champagne.

John Maynard Keynes

As you slide down the banister of life, may the splinters never point in the wrong direction.

Irish blessing

You can spend your whole life trying to be popular, but, at the end of the day, the size of the crowd at your funeral will be largely dictated by the weather.

Frank Skinner

Drama is life with the dull bits cut out.

Alfred Hitchcock

❧

First things first, but not necessarily in that order.

Dr Who

❧

You eat, in dreams, the custard of the day.

Alexander Pope

❧

Man can believe the impossible, but man can never believe the improbable.

Oscar Wilde

❧

I always arrive late at the office, but I make up for it by leaving early.

Charles Lamb

❧

We live in an age when unnecessary things are our only necessities.

Oscar Wilde

❧

I am an optimist. It does not seem too much use being anything else.

Winston Churchill

Sometimes I think we're alone in the universe, and sometimes I think we're not. In either case, the idea is quite staggering.

Arthur C. Clarke

- If you want to end it all, drowning – now, there's a way to go.

- I can't swim.

- Well, you don't have to fuckin' swim, you divvy, that's the whole point. God, you're not very keen, are you?

Dave and Lomper, The Full Monty

The best definition of an immortal is someone who hasn't died yet.

Tom Holt

Self- decapitation is an extremely difficult, not to say dangerous, thing to attempt.

W.S. Gilbert, The Mikado

The fluffy newborn chick of hope tumbles from the eggshell of life and splashes into the hot frying pan of doom.

Humphrey Lyttelton

Death has something to be said for it: There's no need to get out of the bed for it.

Kingsley Amis

People who think there's no good way to die have obviously never heard the phrase "Drug-fuelled-sex heart attack".

Frankie Boyle

- I don't know whether you'll die on the gallows or of the pox.

- That depends, my lord, on whether I embrace your principles or your mistress.

Lord Sandwich and John Wilkes

I am ready to meet my Maker. Whether my Maker is prepared for the great ordeal of meeting me is another matter.

Winston Churchill

Everyone says forgiveness is a lovely idea, until they have something to forgive.

C.S. Lewis

The best measure of a man's honesty isn't his income tax return. It's the zero adjust on his bathroom scale.

Arthur C. Clarke

I was offered the chance to do a tandem skydive, but I draw the line at that. That's no way to die. Imagine my mother at the funeral and the priest saying, "He died as he lived: strapped to another man."

Dara O'Briain

There is nothing quite so good as burial at sea. It's simple, tidy, and not very incriminating.

Alfred Hitchcock

May my last breath be drawn from a pipe and exhaled in a pun.

Charles Lamb

KNOWLEDGE & EDUCATION

Writing – The dawn of legibility in your son's handwriting reveals his total inability to spell.

Geography – He does well to find his way home.

Swimming – Tends to sink.

Arthur Marshall's school report

Everybody who is incapable of learning has taken to teaching.

Oscar Wilde

I recently asked a student where his homework was. He replied, 'It's still in my pencil.'"

Larry Timmons.

An intellectual is a person who's found one thing that's more interesting than sex.

Aldous Huxley

He shows great originality, which must be cured at all cost.

Peter Ustinov's school report

Intelligence was a deformity which must be concealed; a public school taught one to conceal it as a good tailor hides a paunch or a hump.

Cyril Connolly

I am so clever that sometimes I don't understand a single word of what I am saying.

Oscar Wilde

He pursued his studies but never overtook them.

H.G. Wells

Education: the inculcation of the incomprehensible into the indifferent by the incompetent.

John Maynard Keynes

There are only two kinds of people who are really fascinating: people who know absolutely everything and people who know absolutely nothing.

Oscar Wilde

It is bad enough to know the past; it would be intolerable to know the future.

W. Somerset Maugham

The exquisite art of idleness, one of the most important things that any university can teach.

Oscar Wilde

The trouble with the world is that the stupid are cocksure and the intelligent are full of doubt.

Bertrand Russell

It was revealed to me many years ago with conclusive certainty that I was a fool and that I have always been a fool. Since then, I have been as happy as any man has the right to be.

Alistair Sim

A Master of Art is not worth a fart.

Andrew Boorde, 1690

❦

Logic, like whisky, loses its beneficial effect when taken in too large quantities.

Lord Dunsany

❦

You must have taken great pain, sir; you could not have naturally been so stupid.

Samuel Johnson

❦

Never seem more learned than the people you are with. Wear your learning like a pocket watch and keep it hidden. Do not pull it out to count the hours, but give the time when you are asked.

Lord Chesterfield

❦

The avoidance of taxes is the only intellectual pursuit that still carries any reward.

John Maynard Keynes

❦

WEATHER & NATURE

Whenever people talk to me about the weather, I always feel certain that they mean something else.

Oscar Wilde

No, I can't do with mountains at close quarters – they are always in the way, and they are so stupid, never moving and never doing anything but obtrude themselves.

D. H. Lawrence

The climate of England has been the world's most powerful colonizing influence.

Russell Green

Thunder is the sound of God moving his beer barrel across the floor of the sky.

Cyril Fletcher

A few summers like this and we'll all be behaving like Italians.

John Mortimer

We will never be content until each man makes his own weather and keeps it to himself.

Jerome K. Jerome

CLASS & ROYALTY

Put three Englishmen on a desert island and within an hour they'll have invented a class system.

Alan Ayckbourn

When Tommy Cooper was introduced to the Queen at the end of a Royal Variety Performance, he asked her, "Do you like football, ma,'m?" "No," came the reply. "In that case," said Tommy, "can I have your tickets to the Cup Final?"

Bob Monkhouse

I think factories would close down, really, if it wasn't for working-class people.

Victoria Wood

What I want to know is: what is actually wrong with an elite?

Prince Charles

When everyone is somebody, then no one's anybody.

W.S. Gilbert

Important families are like potatoes. The best parts are underground.

Francis Bacon

All castles had one major weakness. The enemy used to get in through the gift shop.

Peter Kay

AGE

Every morning, when you are 93, you wake up and say to yourself, "What, again?"

Ben Travers

We are happier in many ways when we are old than when we were young. The young sow wild oats, the old grow sage.

Winston Churchill

Middle age is that time in life when children and parents cause equal amounts of worry.

Romy Halliwell

Growing old is like being increasingly punished for a crime you haven't committed.

Anthony Powell

I am far too old to retire.

Arthur Lunn, aged 90

Age is just a number. It's totally irrelevant unless, of course, you happen to be a bottle of wine.

Joan Collins

He was 50. It's the age when clergymen first begin to be preoccupied with the underclothing of little schoolgirls in trains.

Aldous Huxley

I'm now at the age where I've got to prove that I'm just as good as I never was.

Rex Harrison

One of the two things that men who have lasted for one hundred years always say: either that they have drunk whisky and smoked all their lives, or that neither tobacco nor spirits ever made the slightest appeal to them.

E.V. Lucas

I attribute my longevity to constant smoking and Marron glacés.

Noel Coward

The greatest problem about old age is the fear that it might go on too long.

A.J.P. Taylor

- One lives and learns, doesn't one?

- That is certainly one of the more prevalent delusions.

Noel Coward, Nude with Violin

One evil of the old age is that you think every little illness is the beginning of the end. When a man expects to be arrested, every knock on the door is an alarm.

Sydney Smith

Inside every old person is a young person wondering what happened.

Terry Pratchett

AMERICA

The difference between England and America is this: when we have a world series, we ask other countries to participate.

John Cleese

In Washington, the first thing people tell you is what their job is. In Los Angeles you learn their star sign. In Houston, you're told how rich they are. And in New York, they tell you what their rent is.

Simon Hoggart

If our Founding Fathers wanted us to care about the rest of the world, they wouldn't have declared their independence from it.

Stephen Colbert

In America, through the pressure of conformity, there is freedom of choice, but nothing to choose from.

Peter Ustinov

Washington is a city of Southern efficiency and Northern charm.

President John F. Kennedy

Actually, American football is somewhat like rugby. But why do they have all those committee meetings?

Winston Churchill

Americans call it The Tonight Show so they can remember when it's on.

Jo Brand

The United States, I believe, is under the impression that they are 20 years in advance of Britain, whilst, as a matter of actual verifiable fact, of course, they are just about six hours behind it.

Harold Hobson

Disney World has acquired by now something of the air of a national shrine. American parents who don't take their children there sense obscurely that they have failed in some fundamental way, like Muslims who never made it to Mecca.

Simon Hoggart

England and America are two countries divided by a common language.

George Bernard Shaw

Soccer? For Americans, it's "a strange sport played by damaged people".

Robin Williams

You can always trust the Americans. In the end, they will do the right thing after they have eliminated all the other possibilities.

Winston Churchill

That seems to point up a significant difference between Europeans and Americans. A European says, "I can't understand this, what's wrong with me?" An American says, "I can't understand this, what's wrong with him?"

Terry Pratchett

Barack Obama will appeal to both black and white voters in America. White voters who'll think he's Tiger Woods.

Frankie Boyle

Americans adore me and will go on adoring me until I say something nice about them.

George Bernard Shaw

MILITARY

The best defense against the atom bomb is not to be there when it goes off.

British Army journal, 1949

He only went into the Army to put his mustache to good purpose.

Alan Bennett

The belief in the possibility of a short decisive war appears to be one of the most ancient and dangerous of human illusions.

Robert Lynd

War does not determine who is right – only who is left.

Bertrand Russell

- Well, Captain. I've got to admire your balls.

- Perhaps later.

Corporal Perkins and Captain Blackadder, Blackadder Goes Forth

Overpaid, overfed, oversexed, and over here.

Tommy Trinder on American forces

I think Iran and Iraq had a war simply because their names are so similar they kept getting each other's post.

Paul Merton

Would you mind awfully falling into three lovely lines?

Sergeant Wilson, Dad's Army

Always forgive your enemies – nothing annoys them so much.

Oscar Wilde

RELIGION

Bishops tend to live a long life – apparently, the Lord is not all that keen for them to join him.

Sir Humphrey Appleby, Yes, Prime Minister

I asked God for a bike, but I know God doesn't work that way. So I stole a bike and asked for forgiveness.

Emo Philips

The only people who still call hurricanes acts of God are the people who write insurance forms.

Neil deGrasse Tyson, astrophysicist.

To put one's trust in God is only a longer way of saying that one will chance it.

Samuel Butler

In Heaven an angel is nobody in particular.

George Bernard Shaw

The more I study religions the more I am convinced that man never worshipped anything but himself.

Richard Francis Burton

Just think what Jesus could have achieved if he'd only had the money.

Michael Bradley

For most people the Church has become little more than a useful landmark by which to offer directions.

The Archbishop of York

Hell is an all-male black-tie dinner of chartered accountants which goes on for eternity.

John Mortimer

I am at peace with God. My conflict is with Man.

Charlie Chaplin

How can what an Englishman believes be heresy? It is a contradiction in terms.

George Bernard Shaw

There are some things only intellectuals are crazy enough to believe.

George Orwell

If God had been a liberal, we wouldn't have had the Ten Commandments – we'd have the Ten Suggestions.

Malcolm Bradbury

We have no reliable guarantee that the afterlife will be any less exasperating than this one, have we?

Noel Coward

The last dream of bliss: staying in Heaven without God there.

Geoffrey Madan

I once asked a Jesuit priest what was the best short prayer he knew. He said,

"'Fuck it', as in, 'Fuck it; it's in God's hands'."

Anthony Hopkins

The end... almost!

Reviews are not easy to come by. As an independent author with a tiny marketing budget, I rely on readers, like you, to leave a short review on Amazon. Even if it's just a sentence or two!

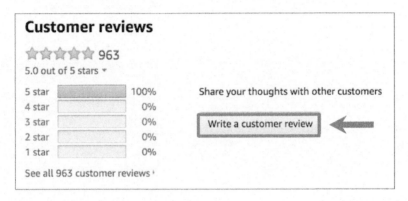

So if you enjoyed the book, please...

>> Click here to leave a brief review on Amazon.

I am very appreciative for your review as it truly makes a difference. Many thanks for purchasing this book and reading it to the end!

SUCCESS & FAILURE

Success is the ability to go from one failure to another with no loss of enthusiasm.

Winston Churchill

Winning is everything. The only ones who remember when you come second are your wife and dog.

Damon Hill

I attribute my whole success in life to a rigid observance of the fundamental rule – never have yourself tattooed with any woman's name, not even her initials.

P.G. Wodehouse

What annoys me about Britain is the rugged will to lose.

William Camp

My friends, as I have discovered myself, there are no disasters, only opportunities. And, indeed, opportunities for fresh disasters.

Boris Johnson

You tried your best and you failed miserably. The lesson is 'never try.

Homer Simpson

A failure is like fertilizer; it stinks to be sure, but it makes things grow faster in the future.

Denis Waitley

One British Olympic sports commentator described a UK runner who was lagging far behind the field as "coming in confidently and supremely fit – a gallant sixteenth".

Michael Bentine

Part of me suspects I'm a loser and the other part thinks I'm God Almighty.

John Lennon

If at first you don't succeed, failure might be your style.

Quentin Crisp

The road to success is always under construction.

Lily Tomlin

Printed in Great Britain
by Amazon